Praxis II

Family and Consumer Sciences Practice Questions

Dear Future Exam Success Story

First of all, **THANK YOU** for purchasing Mometrix study materials!

Second, congratulations! You are one of the few determined test-takers who are committed to doing whatever it takes to excel on your exam. **You have come to the right place.** We developed these practice tests with one goal in mind: to deliver you the best possible approximation of the questions you will see on test day.

Standardized testing is one of the biggest obstacles on your road to success, which only increases the importance of doing well in the high-pressure, high-stakes environment of test day. Your results on this test could have a significant impact on your future, and these practice tests will give you the repetitions you need to build your familiarity and confidence with the test content and format to help you achieve your full potential on test day.

Your success is our success

We would love to hear from you! If you would like to share the story of your exam success or if you have any questions or comments in regard to our products, please contact us at **800-673-8175** or **support@mometrix.com**.

Thanks again for your business and we wish you continued success!

Sincerely,
The Mometrix Test Preparation Team

TABLE OF CONTENTS

Practice Test #1

1. Among these food preparation factors, which can cause food poisoning or other food-borne illness?

a. All of these can cause it with certain foods.
b. Cooking foods for the wrong lengths of time
c. Cooking foods at the wrong temperatures
d. Not pasteurizing or refrigerating some foods

2. How do banks and lenders use credit scores to determine creditworthiness?

a. They show how much money the consumer has available to cover the risk
b. They provide recent historical data of the consumer's use of credit
c. It is an insurance policy if the consumer defaults on a debt
d. They document the consumer's use of credit over the span of their lifetime

3. Who founded the American Association of Family and Consumer Sciences?

a. Mildred Chamberlain
b. Elizabeth C. Stanton
c. Susan B. Anthony
d. Ellen H. Richards

4. Among family roles identified by Virginia Satir, which of these is considered healthy and effective?

a. Blaming others
b. None of these
c. Pleasing others
d. Diverting others

5. To a newborn infant, which of Maslow's levels of needs is most important?

a. Love, belonging
b. Safety, security
c. Self-actualizing
d. Physiological

6. What is correct regarding Freud's and Erikson's theories of development relative to the life span?

a. Freud's theory does not cover the entire life span, but Erikson's does.
b. Erikson's theory does not cover the entire life span, but Freud's does.
c. Neither Freud nor Erikson covered the entire life span in either theory.
d. Both Freud's and Erikson's theories do encompass the entire life span.

7. Which of the following can NOT be achieved through a healthy diet?

a. Improving cholesterol
b. Lowering the risk of type one diabetes
c. Lowering the risk of stroke
d. Reducing blood pressure

8. Which of the following is the most accurate definition of opportunity cost?

a. What you get from giving up something else
b. What you have to give up to get something
c. An exchange, always measurable as money
d. The dollar price to buy a specific opportunity

9. What is the best way to sort clothing in the closet to find items and assemble outfits easily?

a. Sort first by colors, and then sort second by category.
b. Sort by placing favorite items to be most within reach.
c. Sort by placing item types wherever they will fit best.
d. Sort first by category, and then sort second by colors.

10. Regarding nonverbal forms of communicating, which statement is most accurate?

a. Messages conveyed via nonverbal means are not found as truthful as verbal messages are.
b. The use of humor in speaking is not included among the areas of nonverbal communication.
c. Increasing globalization means that nonverbal communication is more universally the same.
d. Increasing globalization requires more awareness, observation, and sensitivity of speakers.

11. Which of the following garments would be the most resistant to wrinkles?

a. Rayon jacket
b. Cotton t-shirt
c. Silk shirt
d. Wool pants

12. Family therapist Virginia Satir identified five common roles of family members. She described only Levelers, who communicate their true feelings honestly, as healthy because their outward communication is congruent with their inward emotions. Which of the other four dysfunctional roles hopes to be loved by being perceived as harmlessly endearing?

a. Blamers
b. Placators
c. Distractors
d. Computers

13. In the realty market, in most US states a "first-time buyer" means:

a. Anyone who has never owned real estate property before.
b. Anyone who has only owned property less than six months.
c. Anyone who has not owned property in the last three years.
d. Anyone who did own, but does not currently own, property.

14. Which of the following elements most makes the floor plan of a house effective?

a. How people move through it
b. How people use the hallways
c. How it looks from standing up
d. How it looks from sitting down

15. In some models of family life stages, which task is most typical of the "later family life" stage?

a. Helping children develop peer relationships
b. Assuming the care for one's family of origin
c. Reminiscing and integrating life experiences
d. Coping with deaths in one's family of origin

16. A person who is 41 to 100% heavier than his or her ideal weight is

a. mildly obese.
b. osteoporotic.
c. diabetic.
d. moderately obese.

17. Which of the following best represents good advice to job applicants for successful interviews?

a. It is good to back up statements about oneself with specific examples.
b. Direct eye contact with interviewers is intimidating and to be avoided.
c. Be prepared to answer interviewer questions but not to ask questions.
d. If one does not understand a question, do not let on and seem foolish.

18. In management decision-making, managers may evaluate alternatives according to four parameters. Determining whether a company's performance goals can maintain a particular alternative or not reflects which of these parameters?

a. Whether an alternative is legal
b. Whether an alternative is ethical
c. Whether an alternative is practical
d. Whether an alternative is economical

19. When working parents look for services to care for their children, which of these is accurate?

a. Because of recent economic factors, many caregivers are charging higher rates.
b. Grandparent child care is less common with fewer extended families cohabiting.
c. To be competitive, "hybrid" providers offer parents additional services included.
d. Au pairs' wages are a bigger challenge than associated government regulations.

20. When should a home buyer get warranty and insurance coverage for the home?

a. After closing before moving in
b. When making a bid on a house
c. At the closing of the home sale
d. When applying for a mortgage

21. What should students taking occupational family and consumer sciences courses mainly be learning?

a. How to prepare themselves for becoming homeowners
b. How to prepare themselves for careers on a lifelong basis
c. How to prepare themselves for getting paid employment
d. How to prepare themselves for balancing family and work

22. What do wardrobe experts advise to individuals for cleaning out their closets?

a. To get rid of anything they have not worn in more than a year
b. To get rid of anything that does not fit them and keep the rest
c. To get rid of anything and everything meeting all these criteria
d. To get rid of anything that is not suited to their personal styles

23. The synthetic woodwork finish that creates the most durable surface is

a. lacquer.
b. polyurethane.
c. varnish.
d. polyester.

24. Which of the following is considered to be the most important determinant of human comfort in housing?

a. Relative humidity
b. Mean radiant temperature
c. Air temperature
d. Air quality

25. Which of the following forms of insurance related to owning a home covers the loss of personal property in the home?

a. Title insurance
b. Flood insurance
c. Home warranties
d. Homeowners' only

26. In his attachment theory regarding parents and children, John Bowlby defined four elements of attachment. Which of these did he say enables a young child to explore the environment?

a. A secure base
b. The safe haven
c. Separation distress
d. Proximity maintenance

27. In which of Erikson's stages does a child first develop awareness of different social roles in the environment?

a. Trust vs. Mistrust
b. Industry vs. Inferiority
c. Initiative vs. Guilt
d. Identity vs. Confusion

28. What is best for consumers to do when they want to buy a house?

a. Look at homes in the location(s) they prefer the most
b. Let a realtor suggest properties based on their needs
c. They may do one or all of these things as they choose.
d. Look at listings for homes with prices they can afford

29. What do nutrition experts recommend to most people for healthy eating and weight control?

a. Multitasking, i.e., eating while working, driving, etc., aids in losing weight.
b. The kinds of foods people eat are what matter rather than the amounts.
c. When trying to lose weight, people should weigh themselves every day.
d. Most people need to change their lifestyles for permanent weight loss.

30. Which of the following fabric care symbols indicates a garment should be line-dried or hang-dried?

a. A square with diagonal lines in a corner
b. A square with one horizontal line inside
c. A square with three vertical lines inside
d. A square with a horizontal arc at the top

31. Some home construction companies design houses based on certain principles. Which of the following is a general rule reflecting good design principles?

a. There should be only one way to get to the kitchen.
b. It is better to have several ways to get to any room.
c. Traffic patterns going through rooms disrupt activity.
d. Separate rooms look bigger than in open floor plans.

32. Once gross income is calculated, how is net income derived?

a. Add cost of goods sold
b. Subtract current liabilities
c. Multiply by current tax rate
d. Subtract all expenses and deductions

33. Which of the following is true about people's nutritional requirements?

a. Drinking tea or coffee does not affect a person's nutritional requirements.
b. Individual requirements for vitamin D are not affected by where one lives.
c. People who exercise more need more food, but may metabolize it better.
d. Malnutrition is only found to be a problem in today's developing countries.

34. Which of the following most accurately represents a concept of Bandura's social learning theory?

a. Children can learn vicariously by observing and imitating others' behaviors.
b. Children only learn directly through consequences of their own behaviors.
c. Children observe and imitate others' behaviors but do not learn from this.
d. Children learn better from positive reinforcement than from punishment.

35. Learning in the same way as others but at an overall slower rate is *most* descriptive of which developmental disability?

a. The autism spectrum
b. Intellectual disability
c. Sensory impairment
d. A learning disability

36. Which of the following foods is a source of the most vitamin A?

a. Sweet potatoes
b. Animal livers
c. Carrots
d. Kale

37. Which of these correctly relates a stage in each theory to the same age periods and family stages?

a. Freud's Oedipal; Erikson's Autonomy vs. Shame, Doubt; Piaget's Preoperational; Duvall's School Age
b. Freud's Anal; Erikson's Industry vs. Inferiority; Piaget's Formal Operations; Duvall's with Preschoolers
c. Freud's Genital; Erikson's Initiative vs. Guilt; Piaget's Concrete Operations; Duvall's with Teenagers
d. Freud's Oral; Erikson's Basic Trust vs. Mistrust; Piaget's Sensorimotor; Duvall's Families with Infants

38. Which of the following was NOT one of the consumer rights asserted by Presidents Kennedy and Nixon during the 1960s?

a. Right to a safe product
b. Right to affordability
c. Right to redress
d. Right to be heard

39. On her 13th birthday, Mary received a gift of $500 from her aunt. Mary wants to save this money for college, and she is not willing to assume any risk on her investment. Which form of savings will likely yield the highest rate of return with no risk?

a. A savings account
b. Purchase of stock
c. Certificate of deposit
d. Mutual fund

40. Which of the following reflects one of the core values of the AAFCS Code of Ethics?

a. To believe that individuals are the basic units of society
b. To espouse variety in scholarship and lifetime learning
c. To maintain the status quo and avoid frequent changes
d. To compartmentalize approaches to supporting others

41. According to the attachment styles defined by Mary Ainsworth through her Strange Situation experiments, which of these did she observe about separation anxiety in children aged 12–18 months?

a. Children who have secure attachments show distress when their mothers leave the room.
b. Children with insecure-ambivalent attachment show no distress if mother leaves the room.
c. Children with insecure-avoidant attachment show extreme distress at the mother's leaving.
d. Children with secure attachment show higher separation anxiety than insecure-ambivalent.

42. Which of the following is a disadvantage of the laboratory method of learning?

a. The laboratory method uses experience so students learn by doing.
b. The laboratory method enhances learning with multisensory modes.
c. The laboratory method involves more time and expense in learning.
d. The laboratory method gives students preparation directly for living.

43. Which types of fabric are usually most flattering to an overweight body type?

a. Medium-weight fabrics with a flat texture
b. Soft, fine-gauge knits with a cuddly texture
c. Strong, large-gauge knits with nubby texture
d. Smooth, very shiny fabrics like silk or silk-look

44. Of the following, which food preparation(s) is/are LEAST likely to cause food-borne illnesses?

a. Improperly canned or fermented
b. Uncooked, i.e., raw meats/produce
c. Undercooked, i.e., not long enough
d. Overcooked, i.e., cooking too long

45. For financial planning, which of the following should an individual or family do first?

a. Developing what their financial goals will be
b. Identifying alternative actions they will take
c. Evaluating consequences of various actions
d. Determining their current financial situation

46. When a home construction company advertises new homes as "energy-efficient" or "energy-saving," which of these are the houses most likely to be?

a. Houses built using building principles and techniques that are more energy-efficient
b. Houses built in the traditional/standard way but fitted with energy-saving appliances
c. Houses built to minimize impacts on the environment, regardless of costs or comfort
d. Houses built to reduce energy used by electronics, which consume the most energy

47. How did the Morrill Act (1862) further the domestic sciences in America?

a. By funding industrial colleges with a land grant to teach household management to farm wives
b. By funding industrial colleges with a land grant to teach farm husbands agricultural techniques
c. By funding states with equal land grants for founding agricultural colleges, like with the Turner Plan
d. By funding enforcement of a law banning bigamy and limiting church/nonprofit land ownership

48. Which of these is true about the %DV (Daily Value) the FDA requires on food labels?

a. They make it easier for consumers to know in numbers how much they need of nutrients in a day.
b. They make it easier for consumers to know how much of a day's allowance of nutrients a food has.
c. They make it harder for consumers to comparison shop for foods by the relative nutrient amounts.
d. They were developed by the FDA to replace RDAs because the RDAs were found to be inaccurate.

49. Some color analysts divide people's coloring into the four seasons for choosing the most flattering palette of colors in clothing and makeup. Others use adjectives associated with temperaments for the same purpose. Which of the following correctly equates these two systems?

a. "Passionate" = "Autumn"; "Dramatic" = "Winter"; "Vibrant" = "Spring"; "Romantic" = "Summer"
b. "Dramatic" = "Autumn"; "Passionate" = "Winter"; "Romantic" = "Spring"; "Vibrant" = "Summer"
c. "Vibrant" = "Autumn"; "Romantic" = "Winter"; "Passionate" = "Spring"; "Dramatic" = "Summer"
d. "Romantic" = "Autumn"; "Vibrant" = "Winter"; "Dramatic" = "Spring"; "Passionate" = "Summer"

50. In textile manufacturing, what is the most accurate definition of the term "gray goods"?

a. Fabrics that have not been dyed
b. Unfinished knit or woven fabrics
c. Fabrics that are not bleached yet
d. Any textile that is gray in its color

51. Research has found which of the following most often?

a. Parents are more likely to expect more of their youngest children.
b. Parents are more likely to expect more from their middle children.
c. Parents are more likely to expect the same from all their children.
d. Parents are more likely to expect more of their firstborn children.

52. The competency, "Apply a variety of assessment methods to observe and interpret children's growth and development" is found under which of the National Standards for Family and Consumer Sciences?

a. Family
b. Human Development
c. Education and Early Childhood
d. Family and Community Services

53. Which of these is most accurate about realtors who help consumers buy homes?

a. Some realtors represent buyers, while others represent sellers.
b. All practicing realtors represent both the buyers and the sellers.
c. Some realtors represent buyers or sellers, while others do both.
d. Whether realtors represent buyers or sellers varies individually.

54. Which of the following more accurately reflects what Bandura believed in developing his social learning theory?

a. The environment an individual is in causes his or her behavior.
b. Environment, behavior, and psychological processes interact.
c. The behavior of an individual creates his or her environment.
d. Psychological processes cause the environment and behavior.

55. Which of these vitamins build up to harmful levels in the body if too much are ingested?

a. Vitamins C and D
b. Vitamins A, D, E, K
c. Vitamin B complex
d. Vitamins never do

56. In fabric that is woven using a triaxial weave, what is the third set of yarn called?

a. The warp
b. The weft
c. The whug
d. The woof

57. Which of the following is NOT a purpose or outcome of the laboratory method of instruction?

a. Students gain motivation through their hands-on experience in the lab.
b. Students gain opportunities for direct participation in original research.
c. Students gain skills in using the laboratory equipment and instruments.
d. Students gain the ability to take lecture notes in the form of an outline.

58. Which of the following disorders *always* involves bingeing and purging by definition?

a. Neither one
b. Anorexia
c. Bulimia
d. Both

59. Which of the following is an example of a consumer responsibility?

a. To make one's concerns heard to those who can address the concerns
b. To have one's voice heard about product development and lawmaking
c. To be able to choose among an abundant variety of goods and services
d. To access information that assures the veracity of product statements

60. Which of these is most realistic about analyzing financial values and developing financial goals?

a. Other people cannot recommend any financial goals for an individual.
b. Other people should advise an individual of goals and which to pursue.
c. Individuals must decide for themselves which financial goals to pursue.
d. Financial goals should include saving and investing but never spending.

61. Why is it important for investors to diversify their investment portfolios?

a. Diversified investments are protected, even if the entire market drops
b. Some of the investments may have a guaranteed return, while others may not
c. Diversified portfolios do not need to be watched as carefully
d. A variety of investments can offset risk

62. What is the first step a person should take toward eliminating wasted time?

a. Keeping a log of how time is spent
b. Resolving to sleep less
c. Purchasing efficient home appliances
d. Using an egg timer

63. What information is required by law for Nutrition Facts panels on food packaging to include?

a. Serving size, number of servings, and calories per serving
b. Amounts of protein, carbohydrates, and fats per serving
c. Fiber, sodium, vitamins, and minerals are not necessary.
d. All of these and more information are required by law.

64. Which special resource(s) would most likely be needed by someone with spina bifida?

a. A communication board
b. Text-to-speech software
c. A wheelchair or crutches
d. Cochlear implantation(s)

65. In making good consumer decisions, which of the following should smart shoppers do first?

a. Narrow the field of potential choices
b. List attributes of products or services
c. Determine their needs as consumers
d. The order of doing these is irrelevant.

66. What is the Betty Lamp?

a. A modern lighting innovation
b. A colonial lighting appliance
c. It was (B) and is also now (D)
d. The symbol of the AAFCS

67. Which of the following solutions would be most practical in housing for a family?

a. Moving to other houses as children grow older
b. Remodeling the house as family needs change
c. A house having some rooms with flexible uses
d. Parents get an apartment when children move

68. One factor that influences consumers to consider prices more in their health care decisions is:

a. When they have no prior ideas of provider quality.
b. When their health insurance plan is a PPO or HMO.
c. When they have a severe and/or urgent condition.
d. When they have health care practitioners they like.

69. In interior design, the arrangement of elements in a pattern around some central point is known as

a. symmetrical balance.
b. gradation balance.
c. asymmetrical balance.
d. radial balance.

70. According to Urie Bronfenbrenner's ecological systems theory of development, in which system does an individual experience the most interpersonal and social interactions?

a. The exosystem
b. The mesosystem
c. The macrosystem
d. The microsystem

71. What are some important skills that FCS graduates specializing in fashion design and interior design need to have for working on design teams or operating, managing, and/or owning private design businesses?

a. Their technical knowledge is more important than their creative abilities.
b. They need business expertise, as well as all skills named in these choices.
c. Having global awareness is more important than expertise with business.
d. Creative abilities are imperative whereas other skills are not as important.

72. In which of Erikson's stages of development do individuals measure their success by what they contribute to their families and society?

a. Intimacy vs. Isolation
b. Ego Integrity vs. Despair
c. Identity vs. Role Confusion
d. Generativity vs. Stagnation

73. When a parent is widowed or divorced, toddlers may react more to:

a. Options (B) and (C) both rather than option (D) only.
b. Changes in familiar routines than the loss of a parent.
c. How that parent copes than loss of the other parent.
d. Parent loss than parental coping or changed routines.

74. Which of the following vitamins is known to improve the body's ability to use phosphorus and calcium?

a. Vitamin E
b. Vitamin D
c. Vitamin B-3
d. Vitamin K

75. Which of these cooking methods is the most energy-efficient?

a. A microwave oven
b. A convection oven
c. An electric oven
d. A gas oven

76. Which of the following nutrients is commonly associated with an increased risk of hypertension?

a. Calcium
b. Fiber
c. Vitamin D
d. Sodium

77. The FCCLA (Family, Career and Community Leaders of America) student organization helps its members to develop personally through Family and Consumer Sciences education and several areas, e.g., character development and creativity. Among four other areas, which is reflected in a student's evaluating several different insurance policies on multiple features and selecting the most suitable one?

a. Career preparation
b. Critical thinking skill
c. Practical knowledge
d. Interpersonal communication

78. What can cause some kinds of dough to become tough?

a. Overhandling any fat-based pastry or cookie dough
b. Pinching buttery pastry edges with warm fingers
c. Overhandling candy clay made using chocolate
d. Putting very wet filling into a pie crust dough

79. As two separate ways of improving decision-making in management, what is a major difference between devil's advocacy and dialectic inquiry?

a. Alternative reassessments
b. The number of alternatives
c. Acceptance of alternatives
d. Effects of greater diversity

80. Which is true about integrating FCS with other academic areas of the curriculum?

a. Historically, curricular deficits developed from the separation of academic and vocational courses.
b. Historically, curricular deficits developed from the separation of college/non-college preparations.
c. Regarding integration of FCS and other CTE courses with academics in curriculum, these are all true.
d. Many State Common Core Standards now integrate career and technical education with academics.

81. The Family, Career and Community Leaders of America (FCCLA) has a mission to use Family and Consumer Sciences education to further personal growth and development in students. Its members develop life skills focused on several roles. Which of the following is NOT one of these roles?

a. Wage earners
b. Family members
c. Business owners
d. Community leaders

82. The AAFCS supports the FCS profession. What is true about its leadership?

a. It works to enhance the well-being of individuals, families, and communities.
b. It influences consumer use of goods and services but not their development.
c. It has a vision and mission to shape social change but not specific public policy.
d. It works to supply leadership to consumers and professionals in all these areas.

83. Among the things parents provide for their children, which would be at the bottom of the pyramid in Maslow's hierarchy of needs?

a. Giving love, ensuring they feel they belong
b. Ensuring they get adequate food and sleep
c. Making sure they have shelter and security
d. Building self-esteem and feelings of worth

84. A business owner decides to invest personal cash into the business. How does this affect the accounting equation?

a. Assets will increase, liabilities will increase, owner's equity will increase
b. Assets will increase, liabilities will decrease, owner's equity will increase
c. Assets will increase, liabilities remain the same, owner's equity will increase
d. Assets will remain the same, liabilities will remain the same, owner's equity will increase

85. For trustworthy online sources of quality health information, what is NOT recommended by the FTC?

a. Websites of federal government agencies
b. Disease-specific nonprofit group websites
c. Search engine results on any health topics
d. Medical school and/or university websites

86. In describing high-context vs. low-context styles of communication, what do "sender-oriented values" mean?

a. The speakers do not consider the values of the listeners.
b. The speaker has responsibility for clearly communicating.
c. The speaker lets listeners be responsible to understand.
d. The speaker uses indirect patterns of verbal orientation.

87. What is true about the USDA's Food Pyramid?

a. MyPyramid was replaced by MyPlate by the USDA in 2011.
b. MyPyramid is the current government food group symbol.
c. MyPyramid and MyPlate both have the same food groups.
d. MyPyramid had fewer food groups than MyPlate includes.

88. Which of the following vitamins is water-soluble?

a. Vitamin D
b. Vitamin E
c. Vitamin A
d. Vitamin C

89. Which of the following includes the consumer's right to a healthy environment?

a. The Consumer Product Safety Commission
b. The UN Consumer Protection Guidelines
c. The Underwriters' Laboratories
d. The Bureau of Competition

90. In household management, which of the following would be the first step to take in the process of solving a problem?

a. To identify alternatives among actions
b. To predict outcomes of various actions
c. To collect data concerning the problem
d. To identify what the problem actually is

91. What percentage of total calorie consumption should be from fat?

a. 10–35 percent
b. 20–35 percent
c. 10–25 percent
d. 20–30 percent

92. When used for weight management, which component of cognitive-behavioral therapy (CBT) is most reflected in a person's not eating in certain environments?

a. Positive self-statements
b. Readiness for change
c. Breaking linkages
d. Self-monitoring

93. An engineer at an automobile manufacturer discovers a potential issue with the engines of the latest model of cars being produced. The flaw could cause the engine to overheat and catch fire. The engineer brings this issue to the attention of management, but they decide that the likelihood of the engine catching fire is low enough that it does not justify the expense of repairing the cars already produced. However, they agree to adjust the engines on all cars being produced going forward. Which of consumer rights is this company failing to meet?

a. Access to information
b. Marketing transparency
c. Product liability
d. Consumer guarantee

94. Housing and Interior Design is Area of Study 11.0 of the National Standards for Family and Consumer Sciences. In this area, Content Standard 11.3 is "Apply housing and interior design knowledge, skills, and processes to meet specific design needs." Of the following competencies, which one falls under this Content Standard?

a. "Critique design plans to address client's needs, goals, and resources.
b. "Describe features of furnishings that are characteristic of various historical periods."
c. "Demonstrate measuring, estimating, ordering, purchasing, pricing, and repurposing skills."
d. "Demonstrate procedures for reporting and handling accidents, safety, and security incidents."

95. A business owner is interested in expanding the product line that her business sells. She wants to make sure that her business has the funds to expand the product line. Which calculation would be the most useful for her?

a. Enterprise budget
b. Free cash flow
c. Capital expenditures
d. Net income

96. Stan owns and operates a printing shop which has been open for 2 years. The shop has been mostly successful, but Stan is barely breaking even at the end of the fiscal year. He believes that a new, top-of-the-line printer will bring in new clientele and greatly increase his revenue. He needs to raise the capital required to purchase the new printer. Which of the following would be the most likely source of capital to pay for the new printer?

a. Bank loan
b. Venture capitalist
c. Crowdfunding
d. Bootstrapping

97. Which kind of oil is NOT an unsaturated fat?

a. Corn oil
b. Olive oil
c. Canola oil
d. Palm oil

98. In order to reduce the risk of spinal bifida in infants, food manufacturers have begun adding

a. calcium.
b. folic acid.
c. iron.
d. vitamin K.

99. What is the major benefit of vitamin A?

a. It helps form new cells.
b. It helps protect the body from disease.
c. It can increase a person's concentration and alertness.
d. It can give a person healthy hair and skin.

100. When a consumer hires a realtor to help in buying a home, which information that the realtor gives the consumer is most important for the realtor to update regularly?

a. The current market conditions
b. Various options for financing
c. All these should be updated
d. Specific negotiating methods

101. The AAFCS Code of Ethics holds members responsible for actively avoiding exploiting people with whom they work or interact professionally. In which category of professional practice does the AAFCS place this principle?

a. Professional Competence
b. Respect for Diversity
c. Conflict of Interest
d. Confidentiality

102. Before the home economics movement began, who of the following pioneered domestic sciences?

a. Both Catherine Beecher and Harriet Beecher Stowe did this.
b. Educator Catherine Beecher, sister of Harriet Beecher Stowe
c. *Uncle Tom's Cabin* author and activist, Harriet Beecher Stowe
d. Neither Catherine Beecher nor Harriet Beecher Stowe did this.

103. A child whose developmental tasks include learning to play in groups, to identify as a female or male, and to have a basic understanding of right and wrong is typically in which life stage?

a. The toddler years
b. Early school years
c. Middle school age
d. Birth to two years

104. Area of Study 12.01 of the Family and Consumer Sciences National Standards is Human Development. In this area, Content Standard 12.1 is: "Analyze principles of human growth and development across the life span." Which of the following Human Development Competencies falls under this Content Standard?

a. "Analyze the effect of heredity and environment on human growth and development."
b. "Analyze the effects of gender, ethnicity, and culture on individual development."
c. "Analyze physical, emotional, social, spiritual, and intellectual development."
d. "Analyze the role of communication on human growth and development."

105. Regarding financial institutions, what is the current status of careers for FCS graduates?

a. Brokerage firms want to hire qualified financial planners, who are among FCS graduates.
b. Banks and savings and loan associations are not presently accepting many job applicants.
c. FCS financial planners are needed at insurance companies but not at counseling agencies.
d. FCS financial planners need not understand community relationship and family dynamics.

106. Of the following AAFCS resolutions related to public legislation, which is the most recent?

a. Life & Career Choices Class Requirement
b. The resolution about Basic Health Literacy
c. The resolution regarding Healthy Weight
d. 10th anniversary of UN Year of the Family

107. Which fabrication method, typical of outerwear, involves stitching a liner fabric in between two outer fabrics?

a. Knitting
b. Stitch-through
c. Quilting
d. Tufting

108. Regarding needs parents must meet for children, which of the following is correct according to the hierarchy of needs Abraham Maslow proposed in his humanistic theory of motivation and personality?

a. Parents must make children feel they are loved before worrying about their feeding and rest.
b. Enabling children to fulfill their highest potentials in life takes precedence over all other needs.
c. Before they can keep children safe, parents must see they get enough water, food, and sleep.
d. Parents should promote children's self-esteem first and then their family acceptance and love.

109. Which of the following foods is classified in two food groups by the US Department of Agriculture (USDA)?

a. Legumes
b. Seafood
c. Cheese
d. Eggplant

110. The nutritional requirements of women:

a. Differ from the requirements of men.
b. Are accurately described by all these.
c. Vary throughout the menstrual cycle.
d. Differ when pregnant and/or nursing.

111. During early childhood, children need more ______ in their diets than older children and most adults do.

a. Magnesium
b. Calcium
c. Potassium
d. Starches

112. What do interpreter-sensitive values mean relative to communication styles?

a. The listener is expected to be responsible for interpreting meaning.
b. The speaker is expected to be responsible for giving a clear message.
c. The speaker avoids nonverbal behaviors for the listener to interpret.
d. The listener need not "read between the lines" as decoding is simple.

113. Which fabric is best for blocking sunlight?

a. Green satin
b. Black cotton
c. White cotton
d. Black satin

114. The AAFCS expects its members to adhere to its professional conduct principle of Integrity. Which of the following reflects this principle?

a. Protecting private information
b. Making ethically sound decisions
c. Practicing within expertise limits
d. Treating consumers with fairness

115. Which of the following is accurate regarding future careers for FCS majors?

a. Accelerating social change causes stress, reducing need for human services administration.
b. Jobs in wellness, long-term health care administration, and dependent care remain stable.
c. More employment opportunities are now developing in the appliance and food industries.
d. There is currently a decrease in the hotel, motel, travel, tourism, and restaurant industries.

116. Which of the following events decreases metabolism?

a. Rapid weight loss
b. Increase in muscle mass
c. Slow weight gain
d. Moderate workout

117. A family wherein the parents, children, and grandmother live together is defined as a(n):

a. Nuclear family
b. Extended family
c. Blended family
d. Combined family

118. In which layout pattern are spaces arranged along a linear path, with major elements at either end?

a. Radial layout
b. Dumbbell layout
c. Clustered layout
d. Doughnut layout

119. Borrowers with a poor credit rating will not be eligible for a bank's

a. prime rate.
b. savings deposits.
c. demand deposits.
d. deposit insurance.

120. Among the following, which is an example of a consumer right?

a. Minimizing environmental impacts through purchasing choices
b. Following safety instructions to ensure the safe use of products
c. Sustainable consumption that will not impinge on others' needs
d. Accessing information that supports better purchasing decisions

Answer Key and Explanations for Test #1

1. A: Food poisoning can be caused by all of these preparation factors with certain foods. For example, cooking for the wrong lengths of time (B) and/or at the wrong temperatures (C) can cause perfringens food poisoning due to the microorganism *clostridium perfringens*. Unpasteurized milk can cause illness from the bacteria *campylobacter jejuni; salmonella; E. coli* 0157:H7 infection; and/or *listeria monocytogenes;* and unrefrigerated (or improperly refrigerated) meats, cream pastries, and egg or potato salads with mayonnaise can cause food poisoning from the bacterium *Staphylococcus aureus.*

2. B: A credit score is a numerical representation of a consumer's history with credit. It is based on several factors, including payment history, total debt, length of credit history, types of credit, and new credit. Typically, negative reports on a credit score remain for up to 7 years and are eventually removed. Lenders use the credit score to determine the risk of the consumer defaulting on the loan. The higher the credit score, the more likely a consumer will be approved for lending.

3. D: Ellen H. Richards was the first woman who graduated from Massachusetts Institute of Technology (MIT) and first female professor teaching there. She was an activist, for not only consumer education, but also women's rights, child protection, public health, nutrition, career education, industrial safety, keeping our air, water, and food pure, and applying principles of management and science to families. She formalized the family and consumer sciences profession and founded the AAFCS (originally American Home Economics Association/AHEA). Mildred Chamberlain (A) created the original design of the colonial Betty Lamp the AHEA adopted as its official symbol. Elizabeth C. Stanton (B) and Susan B. Anthony (C) were pioneers of the women's rights and civil rights movements. (Interestingly, their work began in upstate New York, including Seneca Lake and Rochester; the AHEA was founded nearby in Lake Placid, three years after Anthony's death. Ellen Richards died just five years after Anthony. This area was home to many social reform movements during the late 19th and early 20th centuries.)

4. B: Satir identified five common roles adopted by family members instead of their true identities, especially when under stress. Always blaming, criticizing, and finding fault with the others (A) is one such dysfunctional role. Another is always trying to please the others (C) and apologizing. A third is always distracting the others (D) to deflect their attention from emotional concerns. Hence none of these is considered healthy and effective because family members use these behaviors out of low self-esteem to conceal what they are feeling. (A fifth category she described is the "computer," who outwardly denies all emotion in favor of intellectualizing.) According to Satir, only those she called "levelers," i.e., family members who communicate their true feelings honestly, directly, and openly, are interacting in a healthy and effective manner.

5. D: The most basic level of needs is physiological—for water, sleep, food, elimination, etc.—and comes first in Maslow's hierarchy. These are the needs most important to a newborn infant. Maslow's second level of needs is of those for safety and security (B), which become more important to toddlers. His third level is of needs for love and belonging (A), which become important as children grow. As they get older, they also have needs on Maslow's fourth level, for esteem, i.e., respect, self-confidence, and achievement. His fifth and most evolved level is of needs for self-actualization (C), which includes problem-solving, creativity, moral and ethical development, accepting the truth, and realizing one's greatest potentials. (Note: Maslow's needs levels do not depend only on age; adults may experience any level as a priority at any time in life. However, infants are not yet cognitively developed enough to be concerned with the higher levels.)

6. A: While Erikson based his theory on Freud's, one major difference between them is that Freud only included stages of development through adolescence, whereas Erikson included stages of development through old age until death. Freud considered the personality to be complete by adolescence, but Erikson viewed it as continuing to develop throughout life.

7. B: A healthy diet can lead to improved cholesterol, lower risk of stroke, and reduced blood pressure; however, it has no impact on type one diabetes. There are currently no known prevention measures for type one diabetes.

8. B: The most accurate definition of opportunity cost is what you have to give up to get something else when they may be mutually exclusive financially. For example, someone may be able to attend school part-time while working full-time or work part-time while attending school full-time, or to do each of these part-time; but not to do both full-time. Opportunity cost is not the reverse (A); it represents something lost rather than something gained. While it represents a trade-off, such an exchange is NOT always measurable as amounts of money (C). The cost can be lost time, lost enjoyment, or any other usable benefit(s) lost by choosing an alternative. Opportunity cost does NOT refer to the dollar price of a specific opportunity (D) like college tuition, a mortgage, a car's sticker price, the price for season tickets, etc.

9. D: The most efficient way to sort clothes in the closet for finding them easily is first to sort them by category; e.g., pants all together, shirts all together; for women, skirts all together and dresses all together, etc. After sorting clothing categories, within each category they should then be sorted by color. It is not as easy to find individual items and assemble outfits by sorting into colors first and categories second (A). Putting favorite items most within reach (B) sounds like a good idea if we wear these the most, but is not as efficient as (D). Simply putting things wherever they can most easily be fitted in the closet (C) may be quicker and easier when putting clothes away, but will take longer and be harder to find things when getting dressed.

10. D: While increasing globalization means that cultures are mixing and communicating more, this does not mean that nonverbal forms of communication have become more universally similar (C). It means rather that people are exposed to more culturally dissimilar forms of nonverbal communication, requiring speakers to become more aware, observant, and sensitive to these cultural differences. People generally assume nonverbal communication to be more truthful than verbal communication, not vice versa (A). Humor *is* classified among the major areas of nonverbal communication (B), as are areas like paralinguistics, proxemics, gestures, posture, body language, facial expressions, eye contact, etc.

11. D: Of the given garments, a pair of wool pants would be the most resistant to wrinkles. Because of the thickness of the fiber and the general looseness of the weave, clothing made of wool tends to be very resistant to wrinkles. This is one reason why wool clothing is so useful for travel; it can be packed in a suitcase and not need to be ironed later. Silk and cotton products are moderately resistant to wrinkles. If packed properly, they can be worn without needing to be ironed. Rayon and linen are notoriously prone to wrinkles. Clothing made of these materials must be washed, dried, and stored properly.

12. C: Distractors are described by Satir as those members who divert the others' attention from problematic issues and the attendant emotions by engaging in various attention-getting behaviors. Distractors may be the "babies" of their families, and feel the others will only love them if perceiving them as harmless and cute. Blamers (A) hide their insecurities by attacking the others. Placators (B) try to appease the others to avoid the rejection or disapproval they fear. Computers

(D) avoid confronting or expressing feelings by denying all emotion and limiting their communication to only intellectual, objective, or factual topics.

13. C: One might assume that the term "first-time buyer" refers to anybody who has never owned any real property before (A), but this is not true in the realty market. In most US states, this term actually refers to anyone who has not owned property within the past three years. It does not refer to anyone who has owned real estate property for less than six months (B), or to anyone who once owned but does not currently own any real estate property (D).

14. A: The traffic patterns in the floor plan of a house, i.e., how people move through it, are what most make the floor plan work well. Expert home builders say that successful floor plans are not determined by how they look to people when they are standing up (C) or sitting down (D), i.e., when they are still; but rather by how easily they navigate the home when they are moving. Some builders design homes where people go through one room to get to another rather than going through hallways (B), because they find this design makes it easier to see throughout the house and gives the effect of larger rooms.

15. C: The "later family life" stage is the last stage of some models (cf. Carter & McGoldrick, 1999; Carr, 2006), when family tasks include coping with physical deterioration in oneself and others and with losing spouses and peers; parents' relinquishing, and adult children's assuming, more responsibility to maintain families; and elder members' reminiscing, reviewing their lives, integrating their life experiences, and preparing for death. Helping children develop relationships with their peers (A) is a typical task of the "family with young children" stage. Assuming care for one's family of origin (B) is typically a task during the "family with adolescents" stage. Coping with deaths in one's family of origin (D) is typically a task involved in the stage of "launching children."

16. D: A person who is 41 to 100% heavier than his or her ideal weight is moderately obese. Health professionals have divided obesity into three degrees: mild, moderate, and severe. A person who is less than 20% heavier than his or her ideal weight is considered merely overweight, but a person who is 20 to 40% heavier is considered mildly obese. People who are more than 100% heavier than their ideal weight are severely obese. Moderately obese people are much more likely to have diabetes or osteoporosis, but do not necessarily suffer from these conditions.

17. A: One good piece of advice for job applicants preparing for interviews is, when answering questions about themselves, they should support statements they make about their own positive attributes with specific examples to illustrate those qualities whenever they can. However, it is not good advice to avoid eye contact with interviewers (B). This would be good advice in Japan, where direct eye contact is found intimidating and is avoided; but in America, it is a sign that one is paying attention and is interested in the conversation. Avoiding eye contact in job interviews in America can be interpreted as a lack of confidence or as dishonesty. Applicants should be prepared not only to answer questions, but also to ask them (C). Applicants can ask interviewers what the company is looking for in an employee; interviewers' responses can provide applicants with opportunities to explain how they meet those needs. If applicants do not understand an interviewer question, they should not try to hide it (D), but rather should request clarification.

18. D: Whether a company's performance goals can support an alternative reflects whether the alternative is economically feasible. Whether an alternative is legal (A) is reflected by whether an alternative is lawful in this country, and in others for companies that export goods or services. Whether it is ethical (B) is reflected if the alternative will not cause undue harm to stakeholders and is morally acceptable. Whether an alternative is practical (C) is reflected by whether the organization's management has the resources and abilities to implement it.

19. C: Due to the recent economic recession (c. 2007–2009), many child caregivers are now offering multiple services, like housekeeping, tutoring, etc. Parents can thus get help in more areas for their money. Also because of the recession, many caregivers are charging *lower* rates, not higher (A). Another recent trend owing to economic factors is *more* parents getting help with child care from their own parents (B). (Fewer extended families lived together in the recent past than historically, but this is changing.) Some families relocate to live with/nearer to their parents, or invite their parents to live with/closer to them. This offers dual advantages of saving money on child care, and helping grandchildren and grandparents get better acquainted. Au pairs, i.e., foreign nationals, typically cost *less* in wages because parents provide their room and board as well, but State Department regulations limit their service to one-year periods, preventing longer-term provider continuity for young children. Hence regulations are a bigger challenge than wages with au pairs, not vice versa (D).

20. C: Home buyers need to get home warranty and insurance coverage at the closing of the sale. Thus they should consult an insurance broker or a realtor before the closing to get information and make choices. It is too late to obtain insurance after the closing (A), but too early when making a bid on a house (B) since the home buyer does not know yet if s/he will end up buying the house when bidding. It would also be premature to obtain insurance when applying for a mortgage (D), which the buyer should do before making an offer for a specific house to the seller.

21. C: Occupational family and consumer sciences courses are mainly for teaching students how to prepare themselves to seek and obtain paying employment, not necessarily for establishing lifelong careers (B). They are not for teaching students how to manage being homeowners (A), or for teaching them how to balance their future family and work lives (D). The focus of occupational FCS programs is to learn and apply FCS skills, knowledge, and attitudes that will help them secure paid jobs.

22. C: Wardrobe experts advise individuals to use "tough love" on their closets and get rid of anything they have not worn for more than a year (A), anything that does not fit them (B), and anything that is not consistent with their personal styles (D) rather than only one of these. For those who can afford it, experts recommend that if they cannot bear to part with many such items and/or have trouble deciding which things to get rid of, to employ a personal stylist for help.

23. D: Polyester is the synthetic woodwork finish that creates a durable surface. It is an opaque finish, meaning that it obscures the natural look of the lumber underneath. Lacquer, polyurethane, and varnish are the other three popular opaque woodwork finishes. Polyurethane is quite durable as well, but it can be difficult to repair when it is damaged. Varnish can be either opaque or transparent; it is usually easier to apply than lacquer. Vinyl is a transparent finish that is resistant to degradation by moisture and chemicals.

24. C: Housing experts consider air temperature to be the most important determinant of human comfort. There are a number of factors that influence human comfort, but the primary concern for most people with regard to housing is to be kept warm and dry. In general, a house needs to be between 69 and 80 degrees Fahrenheit in order for its inhabitants to be comfortable. The other answer choices are other factors that affect comfort. Relative humidity is the moisture content of the air relative to the amount of moisture that could be in the air at that temperature without condensing. People tend to be comfortable in houses that maintain a relative humidity from 30 to 65%. Mean radiant temperature is the degree to which a person's temperature changes because of radiation. Depending on the air temperature and ventilation of a room, the people and objects within it will either absorb or give off heat. It is more comfortable to absorb heat than to lose it. Air quality is the amount of pollutants and noxious vapors in the atmosphere. Obviously, air quality correlates to comfort. Ventilation is the degree to which the air in a room circulates freely. The amount of ventilation appropriate for a room will depend on its intended use. Kitchens and bathrooms, for instance, tend to benefit from more ventilation.

25. B: Flood insurance not only covers the loss of or damage to a home due to flooding; it also covers the loss or damage of personal property and other contents within the home. Title insurance (A) only protects home buyers up to the real estate's mortgage value ("lenders" policies), and protects homeowners up to the purchase price of the home including down payments ("owners" policies) if the title to the real property turns out to be invalid. It does not cover personal property. Home warranties (C) cover workmanship in a new home, usually for the first year; wiring, plumbing, and other mechanical issues for the first two years; and structural defects in the building for up to ten years. They do not cover personal property in the home. Therefore, it is incorrect that homeowners' insurance is the only form of insurance to cover personal property (D).

26. A: Bowlby defined a secure base as the parent or attachment figure, who provides a constant source of security, functioning as the young child's "base" like a base camp or headquarters. Having this secure base enables the child to venture forth to explore the environment with the knowledge that s/he can still return to the base for security rather than lose his/her way. Bowlby defined the safe haven (B) as the child's being able to return to the parent to regain safety and comfort when s/he encounters a threat or feels fear. Bowlby defined separation distress (C) as the anxiety felt by young children when the parent is not there. He defined proximity maintenance (D) as the child's need to be near the parent, and in general the human being's desire to be near other people to whom s/he is attached.

27. C: Erikson's stage of Initiative vs. Guilt occurs during the preschool years of early childhood, when children begin exploring their environments, first develop awareness of the different social roles existing around them, and experience feelings of either purpose and accomplishment or guilt and inhibition. Erikson identified the family as the primary influence on children's development during this stage. Trust vs. Mistrust (A) occurs during infancy, when a baby's needs are either met fully and consistently, engendering feelings that the world can be trusted; or incompletely and/or inconsistently, fostering a general mistrust of people. Industry vs. Inferiority (B) occurs when children start school, their world widens from the family to school and social relationships, and they develop a sense of either mastery or inadequacy.

28. C: According to REALTOR.com, some home buyers prefer to look at listings of homes based on their locations (A); some want to look at listings based on their prices (D); some look at listings based on both their location and pricing criteria; some would rather have a local realtor suggest properties to them according to criteria they have communicated to the realtor (B); and many consumers like to combine these methods to maximize the number of potential properties they can consider. Which approach(es) they choose to look for a home is really up to the consumer.

29. D: Nutrition experts advise people who want to lose weight permanently that they need to change their lifestyles rather than go on and off a diet, which results in regaining any weight lost. They also advise *against* eating while doing other things (A), which does not help in losing weight but more often leads to weight gain as people are not mindful of what and how much they eat or when they are full. While some kinds of foods are better for us than others, portion sizes *do* matter (B). Some foods, e.g., leafy greens, can be eaten in larger quantities than others, e.g., ice cream; but moderation in the amounts we eat overall is best. Experts advise people trying to lose or maintain weight to weigh themselves weekly, not daily (C). Normal daily weight fluctuations from fluids and other factors make true weights unclear; weighing weekly makes it easier to know whether one has lost, gained, or maintained weight.

30. D: The fabric care symbol of a square with an arc resembling a slightly slack clothesline hanging from between the top corners indicates the garment should be line-dried or hang-dried. The symbol of a square with diagonal lines in the upper left corner (A) indicates the garment should be dried in the shade (i.e., not in direct sunlight if this would fade the dye). A square with one horizontal line inside (B) indicates the garment should be dried flat. A square with three vertical lines inside (C) indicates the garment should be drip-dried.

31. B: One design principle embraced by some home design companies is that there should be at least three ways to get to a room in the house. They find this especially important for getting to the kitchen, which is the center of many family homes; therefore (A) is incorrect. Floor plans can be designed wherein people get to different rooms by passing through other rooms in an open floor plan, yet without disrupting how the rooms are used (C). These open floor plans make the rooms look bigger than if they were separated by halls (D) used as passageways. They also make it easier to see farther through the house.

32. D: Gross income equals gross revenue (the total of all monies received and due for goods delivered or services performed) reduced by the cost of goods sold. Net income is the profit (or loss) realized after all expenses and deductions are subtracted. These include administrative costs, operating expenses (e.g., rent and insurance), taxes, and interest.

33. C: People who exercise more do need more calories from food since they burn more; however, exercise also enhances metabolic efficiency in some individuals. Drinking tea and/or coffee *does* affect nutritional requirements (A): both beverages interfere with the absorption of iron and zinc. Vitamin D requirements *are* affected by where one lives (B): people living in the northern half of the United States do not get enough vitamin D through exposure to sunlight during winter. People living south of the 45th parallel, or a line drawn between Atlanta, Georgia, in the east and Los Angeles, California, in the west, have access to strong enough sunlight in winter for sufficient vitamin D, but often lack exposure to sunlight during summers when they stay indoors with air-conditioning to avoid the heat. Malnutrition is a serious problem in developing countries today, but is also an issue in developed countries (D) among people who eat too many overprocessed, refined foods whose nutrients have been removed.

34. A: Bandura discovered that children learn not only from experiencing the consequences of their own behaviors (B), but can also learn vicariously by observing others' behaviors and their consequences, and then imitating those behaviors to obtain similar rewards or avoid similar punishments. In his social learning theory, Bandura proposed that children do indeed learn from observing and imitating others' behaviors (C). The concept that children learn better from positive reinforcement than from punishment (D) is a principle of behaviorism. Bandura's theory uses behaviorist concepts, but adds to behaviorism's idea that learning occurs through environmental consequences of behaviors the social element of observing others' behaviors and their consequences and then imitating them. (Behaviorists have found punishments induce unfavorable reactions threefold over rewards, but positive reinforcements [rewards] are also far more powerful in encouraging desired behaviors than punishments in discouraging undesired behaviors.)

35. B: Intellectual disability is most characterized by learning in the same way as nondisabled peers, but at an overall slower rate. The autism spectrum (A) is more characterized by normal intelligence and learning at a normal rate but with deficits in specific areas, e.g., in social comprehension, range of interests and activities, and verbal communication for some. Sensory impairments (C) do not necessarily cause slower overall learning: deaf children take longer to learn reading specifically because of its strong auditory basis, but they learn language just as quickly provided sign language or other accessible modalities; blind children, given Braille or other methods, do too; and neither deaf nor blind children learn more slowly in other areas. While those with learning disabilities (D) may or may not take longer to learn certain things, they are not intellectually disabled; moreover, they do *not* learn the same way as others, but learn differently in specific areas. They often succeed in these areas if taught differently.

36. B: Liver from any animal has the highest amount of vitamin A, with turkey liver being the highest, providing over 1500% of the Daily Value (DV) per 100-gram (3½-ounce) serving. Sweet potatoes (A) provide 384% of the DV of vitamin A per 100-gram serving. Carrots contain beta-carotene, which is converted by the body to vitamin A, providing 334% of the DV for a 100-gram (raw) serving. Kale (D) provides 308% of the DV of vitamin A per 100-gram serving via its carotenes.

37. D: Freud's Oral stage corresponds to infancy, as does Erikson's stage of Basic Trust vs. Mistrust, Piaget's Sensorimotor stage, and Duvall's Families with Infants stage. Freud's Oedipal stage (A) corresponds to preschool; Erikson's corresponding stage is Initiative vs. Guilt, rather than toddlerhood's Autonomy vs. Shame and Doubt; Piaget's Preoperational stage corresponds to preschool, but Duvall's corresponding stage is Families with Preschoolers, not School Age. Freud's Anal (B) stage corresponds to toddlerhood; Erikson's corresponding stage is Autonomy vs. Shame and Doubt, not Industry vs. Inferiority, which occurs during elementary/middle school ages. Piaget's stages corresponding to toddlerhood are the end of the sensorimotor and beginning of the preoperational, not formal operations, which develops around adolescence. Toddlerhood falls between Duvall's Families with Infants and Families with Preschoolers stages. Freud's Genital (C) stage is in adolescence, as is Duvall's Families with Teenagers, but Erikson's corresponding stage is Identity vs. Role Confusion, not infancy's Basic Trust vs. Mistrust; Piaget's is Formal Operations, not the elementary/middle school years' Concrete Operations.

38. B: Presidents Kennedy and Nixon did not include the right to affordability among the consumer rights asserted during the 1960s. Businesses do not have any obligation to sell products at prices within reach of the average consumer. There were five essential consumer rights promulgated at that time: the right to a safe product; the right to redress; the right to be heard; the right to be informed; and the right to choose. The government enforces laws that require businesses to sell safe products or to clearly warn consumers about products that are not always safe. The right to redress enables consumers to receive a refund or compensation of some kind when a product does them harm. Consumers have a right to speak and be acknowledged by businesses. Consumers also have a right to as much information about products as they desire. Finally, consumers have a right to choose among a variety of products; it is with this in mind that the government enforces laws against monopoly.

39. C: Mary will be saving her money for approximately 5 years. A standard savings account assumes almost no risk, but also will also return a low amount of interest. Stock and mutual funds come with varying rates of risk and return, so this would not be a good option given Mary's unwillingness to assume risk. The best choice would be the certificate of deposit (CD). Mary can decide the length of the term, she will receive a higher interest rate than a standard savings account, and there is very little risk associated with a CD.

40. B: This reflects the AAFCS Code of Ethics' Core Value: "Support life-long learning and diverse scholarship." Other Core Values include: "Believe in the family as a fundamental unit of society"; thus (A) is incorrect; "Seek new ideas and initiatives and embrace change"; hence (C) is incorrect; and "Promote an integrative and holistic approach, aligned with the FCS body of knowledge, to support professionals who work with individuals, families, and communities"; hence (D) is incorrect.

41. A: Ainsworth found in her experiments that children with secure attachments to their mothers showed distress when their mothers left the room. She expanded the work of John Bowlby, who defined separation anxiety as a characteristic of normal attachment. Ainsworth found that children she identified as having insecure-ambivalent attachment showed more extreme distress at their mothers leaving than securely attached children, rather than showing no distress (B). However, she found that children she defined with insecure-avoidant attachment showed no distress upon their mothers' leaving the room, rather than showing extreme distress (C). Therefore, children with secure attachment show normal separation anxiety, but this is a lower level of separation anxiety than the level displayed by children with insecure-ambivalent attachment, not higher (D).

42. C: One disadvantage of instruction using the laboratory method is that lab experiments and other procedures consume more time than other learning methods, and the apparatus used in labs can be very expensive. The experiential nature of the lab method means that students learn by actually doing things instead of by reading about or being told about them, which is an advantage (A). Students generally learn better when they receive material through multiple sensory modalities; this is another advantage of the lab method (B). An additional advantage of the lab method is that through hands-on experience and discovery, it prepares students directly for many processes they will encounter in real life (D).

43. A: A medium-weight fabric, with just enough stiffness to skim over the body rather than cling to it (but not so stiff as to look boxy), with a flat texture that does not make body parts look bigger, is generally most flattering to overweight body types. Soft, fine-gauge knits (B) have a nice cuddly feel, but they cling to the body, showing off every lump and bump, so they are not as flattering to the overweight. Knits of larger gauge yarn with nubby textures (C) make a large body look even larger. Smooth, very shiny fabrics like silk or silky-looking synthetics (D) reflect the light, again making big bodies look bigger; and they may also be clingy.

44. D: Cooking food for too long can burn it or dry it out, causing poor taste and texture and removing nutrients. Grilling or charring foods at high temperatures can cause it to contain carcinogens (cancer-promoting agents), as can burning them; but cancers are not food-borne illnesses, which are caused by viral, bacterial, or parasitic microorganisms present in foods. Improperly canned foods and fermented fish (A) can cause botulism, which can be deadly. Uncooked or raw meats and produce (B) can cause many food-borne illnesses, as can undercooked foods (C).

45. D: The first step in financial planning is to determine what the individual's or family's current financial circumstances are. The second step is to develop what their financial goals will be (A). The third step is to identify different possible actions they may take (B). The fourth step is to evaluate the potential consequences of taking any of those actions among the alternatives (C). Additional steps include making a financial plan of action, implementing it, reevaluating that plan, and changing it as needed.

46. A: Concerns over climate change and protecting our environment has prompted many construction companies to research building science principles to make new houses more energy-efficient. These houses are not built in traditional ways but simply containing energy-saving appliances (B); rather, they reduce the use of energy in the house greatly from the use in a house built, for example, seven years ago. These new houses are built not only to minimize the carbon footprint, i.e., the environmental impact, of those living in them; they are also built to cost homeowners less in energy expenses and to make living there more comfortable for them (C). Building scientists find that heating and cooling are what consume the most energy in houses, not electronics (D).

47. A: The Morrill Act funded land grants to US states to create agricultural colleges. This law did enable these colleges to educate farmers in agricultural techniques (B); however, the way it furthered domestic sciences in America specifically was by enabling these same colleges to educate the farmers' wives in household management (A). The Turner Plan, written by Illinois College's Professor Jonathan Baldwin Turner, gave states equal land grants for agricultural colleges. However, the Morrill Act, also written by Turner and introduced by Vermont congressman Justin Smith Morrill, did *not* allocate *equal* land grants to all states (C), but grants of variable sizes according to how many congressional representatives and senators each state had. This favored the eastern states, which had larger populations. The Morrill *Anti-Bigamy* Act, also passed in 1862 by President Abraham Lincoln, banned bigamy and limited church/nonprofit land ownership (D), targeting the Utah Territory's Mormons; however, its enforcement was *not* funded; Lincoln never enforced it; and it did not further domestic sciences.

48. B: %Daily Values (DVs) make it easier for consumers to know how much of what they need daily of certain nutrients a food supplies. For example, if a food contains 33%DV of sodium, the consumer knows that food supplies 1/3 of the sodium s/he should consume in a day. This means consumers need *not* know the actual numerical amounts of nutrients they need daily, or how much of that number a food has (A); e.g., they need not know that 2400 mg of sodium is how much to consume daily, or that a food with 800 mg of sodium has 1/3 the DV. %DVs also make it *easier* for consumers to comparison shop, not harder (C); e.g., they can pick a food lower in sodium instead of one with too much. The FDA developed DVs *not* because the RDAs were inaccurate (D), but because certain nutrients the FDA wanted to require on labels did not have RDAs established for them.

49. A: Many color analysts use the four seasons to identify the main categories of color palettes. In this system, "Autumn" represents warm, yellow-based earth tones; "Winter" represents cool, blue-based colors and black and white; "Spring" represents bright, vibrant, clear colors; and "Summer" represents soft, light pastel tints of colors. Some color analysts use adjectives descriptive of temperaments for the same groups. In this system, "Passionate" equals "Autumn"; "Dramatic" equals "Winter"; "Vibrant" equals "Spring"; and "Romantic" equals "Summer."

50. B: In textile manufacturing, any knitted or woven fabric that just came off the loom and has not yet been finished is called "gray goods." This includes all fabrics that have not been singed, bleached (C); optically brightened, mercerized, dyed (A); printed, glazed, napped, stonewashed or tumbled; distressed; treated with anti-staining or anti-wrinkling finishes, etc. It does not refer only to gray-colored textiles (D).

51. D: Research studies have consistently found that parents are more likely to expect more from their firstborn children. New parents with no previous experience of having their own children are likely to place higher expectations on their first child. By the time they have had more children and experience, they are likely to lower their expectations of their middle (B) and youngest (A) children to be more realistic. Hence most parents are not likely to have the same expectations of all their children (C).

52. C: The competency quoted is Competency 4.2.2 under Content Standard 4.2, "Analyze developmentally appropriate practices to plan for early childhood, education, and services" under National Standard 4.0, Education and Early Childhood, whose comprehensive standard is, "Integrate knowledge, skills, and practices required for careers in early childhood, education, and services." The standard for Family (A) is National Standard 6.0, whose comprehensive standard is, "Evaluate the significance of family and its effects on the well-being of individuals and society." Human Development (B) is National Standard 12.0, whose comprehensive standard is "Analyze factors that influence human growth & development." Family and Community Services (D) is

National Standard 7.0, whose comprehensive standard is "Synthesize knowledge, skills, and practices required for careers in family & community services."

53. A: In the real estate business, it is most common for some realtors to represent buyers and others to represent sellers. Realtors typically do not represent both {(B), (C)}. This does not typically vary by the individual realtor (D), as realtors usually represent either home buyers or home sellers.

54. B: Traditional behaviorists believed that an individual's environment caused the individual's behaviors (A). Bandura proposed that not only do the individual's behaviors also cause the environment (C), which he *reciprocal determinism;* i.e., the environment and the behaviors mutually determine one another, but moreover that the individual's psychological processes (D) also interact with environment and behavior to produce learning and shape the personality. Thus he did not believe that any one of these factors caused any other(s), but that all three reciprocally interact and influence each other.

55. B: Vitamins A, D, E, and K are fat-soluble vitamins, meaning they dissolve in lipids, i.e., fats. The body absorbs these vitamins in fat globules and stores them in the tissues. Therefore, if someone ingests excessive amounts of any of these vitamins, they can build up to harmful levels. Vitamin C (A) and the complex of B vitamins (C) are water-soluble vitamins, meaning they dissolve in water and are not stored in the tissues. Any excess amounts are excreted in urine and sweat. Water-soluble vitamins do not build up in the body, but fat-soluble vitamins do. Therefore (D) is incorrect.

56. C: Woven fabrics can be made using a plain weave, a twill weave, a satin weave, or a triaxial weave. In the plain weave, one yarn alternates going over and under the other. The two yarns at right angles are called the warp (A) and the weft (B). In the twill weave, the weft goes under and over two or more warp yarns at regular intervals. In the satin weave, each yarn goes over four or more others before crossing under another one. The low twist and long "float," or distance yarn goes between crossings, make satin smooth and shiny. In the triaxial weave, yarns go in three directions instead of only two. In addition to a warp and weft, the third yarn direction is called the whug (C). Woof (D) is not a weaving term. (In audio electronics, e.g., speakers and amplifiers, tweeters transmit high sound frequencies and woofers transmit low frequencies.)

57. D: In the laboratory method of learning, students do not listen to lectures or take notes. Rather, they participate directly in hands-on observations and experiments. These direct experiences often stimulate students' interest and motivation (A) for a subject more than reading textbooks or listening to lectures alone can. The laboratory method also affords students the chance to participate in original research (B), which can be very exciting and can earn them credit and recognition for research in the field of the course they are studying. Moreover, in this method students learn skills for using the instruments and equipment (C) in the lab, a valuable asset for future lab courses, internships, and employment.

58. C: By definition, bulimia is a disorder wherein the patient binge-eats excessive amounts of food and then purges it by inducing vomiting, abusing laxatives, or both. Anorexia (B), a disorder wherein the patient starves, eating almost no food, and often also exercises excessively, *sometimes* but *not always* also includes binge-eating and purging, or just purging. Therefore, (A) and (D) are incorrect.

59. A: Making one's concerns heard to those who can address them is an example of the consumer's responsibility for being heard. Having one's voice heard about product development and lawmaking (B) is an example of the consumer's *right* to be heard. Being able to choose among a variety of goods and services (C) is an example of the consumer's *right* to choice. An example of the consumer's *responsibility* for choice is to exercise due care and caution in choosing from among that variety. Accessing information that assures product statements are true (D) is an example of the consumer's *right* to information. An example of the consumer's *responsibility* regarding information is wisely conducting analyses and applications of the available product information.

60. C: It can help for other people to recommend financial goals (A), especially for young people about to be graduated from high school or college and/or starting jobs. However, though others can give advice about goals, they should not tell the individual which ones to pursue (B); this is something the individuals must decide for themselves. Financial goals can include savings, investments, and spending as well (D). If someone has a goal to buy a house, car, business, etc., these are included as financial goals, so spending can be as much a part of a person's financial goals as saving and/or investing to provide for financial security and/or freedom in the future.

61. D: Diversified portfolios can offset some risk. If one investment is performing poorly, another investment may do very well, making up for any losses. The more varied the industries and characteristics of the investments, the more likely an investor will see an overall increase over time.

62. A: The first step towards eliminating wasted time is to keep a log of how time is spent. In the chaotic modern world, almost everyone feels as if he or she is moving in a dozen different directions at once. The natural result is the creeping suspicion that time is being wasted and maximum productivity is not being achieved. Time management experts agree that the first step in eliminating wasted time is to determine where it is being wasted. This is done by keeping an activity log for several days and then studying it to find where time is typically wasted. Once the time wasters have been identified, it will become easier to tighten up the daily schedule.

63. D: Nutrition Facts panels on food packaging are required by law to include the serving size, number of servings per container, calories per serving; grams of protein, carbohydrates, fats, and fiber per serving; milligrams of sodium per serving; and the percentage per serving of the Daily Value for protein, carbohydrates, fats, cholesterol, and also certain vitamins and minerals.

64. C: Certain types of spina bifida cause paralysis. The vertical location of the defect in spinal column closure dictates how high the paralysis occurs: in some patients the bladder and bowels are affected, while in others it may be limited to the feet and lower legs. A common symptom is inability or difficulty in walking. Communication boards (A) are for people who cannot speak for cognitive (e.g., intellectual disability) or neuromuscular (e.g., cerebral palsy) reasons or vocal system disorders. Text-to-speech software (B) is also for people who cannot speak normally, including those with autistic disorders, deafness, ALS, etc. Cochlear implantations (D) are to restore hearing for those with sensorineural hearing loss.

65. C: The first thing consumers should do before making a decision to purchase goods or services is to identify their needs, e.g., how they will use the product or service; how often; where to store a product; the location of a service. The second thing they should do is to list the attributes they want the product or service to have (B); e.g., a doctor has long enough office visits, short enough patient waiting times, and a good bedside manner; an insurance company settles claims promptly, subrogates effectively, and charges low premiums; or a power tool is cordless, lightweight, and powerful. The third thing is to narrow the field of possible choices (A); e.g., which are available for sale, which have prices the consumer can afford; product support and customer service; and how each choice meets the consumer's needs and desired product/service attributes. Thus the order of these steps is not irrelevant (D).

66. C: The Betty Lamp is not a modern lighting innovation (A). Rather, it was a lamp widely used during colonial times in early America, which gave a relatively good quality of light for the time. Because this lamp was historically used to light not only family life, but also all household industries, and because it could represent the enlightenment that the American Association of Family and Consumer Sciences (AAFCS) is dedicated to providing, the AAFCS adopted it as its official symbol (D) in 1926.

67. C: A design innovation in home construction is including some rooms planned to be flexible in purposes and use. This allows homes to change along with families. For example, when a grown child moves out, that child's bedroom can easily be converted to a home gym, home theater, craft room, etc. As children grow older, a playroom can become a game room, homework/studying room, hobby room, etc. This eliminates having to move to another house (A), which takes more money, time, and effort; and many families love their homes, neighbors, and neighborhoods and do not want to move. Remodeling (B) also costs more, and ongoing work inconveniences home living. While some "empty nest" parents may want to downsize to an apartment (D), this again involves more effort and time, even if proceeds from a house sale cover moving expenses. And some parents want to keep the space in their house for grown children, their families, and others to visit.

68. A: According to research, consumers who have not formed any preconceived notions about the quality of various providers through what they have heard from others, through advertising they have seen/heard, or through their own prior experiences are more interested in price as a factor in their health care decisions. However, when consumers have traditional health insurance plans, like PPOs or HMOs (B), they are less interested in price because these plans control price. When consumers have severe or urgent medical conditions (C), they are less interested in price because obtaining immediate care takes priority. And when they like their current health care practitioners (D), they are less interested in price because they want to see the same provider(s) regardless.

69. D: In interior design, the arrangement of elements in a pattern around some central point is known as radial balance. For instance, a dining room might be arranged such that all of the furniture extends out from a central table. The pattern of the radial elements can be based on size, color, or texture. Symmetrical balance is the arrangement of identical elements around a center point or line. This is the most rigidly balanced form of interior design. Gradation balance is the subtle but regular alteration of specific elements in an interior. For instance, a room might include various shades of the same color. Asymmetrical balance is the arrangement of unlike elements that nevertheless creates a balance when looked at as a whole. Harmonic balance is the agreement of the various design elements in a room. It does not entail any particular physical arrangement.

70. D: What Bronfenbrenner termed the microsystem is a person's immediate environment, including family, friends, communities, religious groups, and others with which the person has direct contact and regular interactions. The exosystem (A) is what Bronfenbrenner named the wider social system of events and experiences that directly affect a person's microsystems but which the person does not construct; e.g., getting or losing a job. The mesosystem (B) is what Bronfenbrenner called the system of connections between elements of the microsystem; e.g., between a child's parents and teachers, friends and relatives, etc. The macrosystem (C) is what Bronfenbrenner labeled the cultural beliefs, values, laws, rules, and customs that influence the person. (Bronfenbrenner also identified the chronosystem, a system in the dimension of time that includes processes and events like biological maturation, parental death, etc.)

71. B: Today's FCS graduates who specialize in fashion and interior design must have a combination of technical knowledge, creative abilities {(A), (D)}, global awareness, and business expertise (C) for working on design teams or operating, managing, and/or owning private design businesses. No one of these is more important than the others.

72. D: Erikson's stage of Generativity vs. Stagnation occurs in middle adulthood, when people focus on creating legacies to leave for future generations, such as children, businesses, homes, inventions, and other contributions to family and society. Those who stagnate rather than generate become self-absorbed. Intimacy vs. Isolation (A) occurs in young adulthood, when people either succeed at forming intimate relationships with others or become isolated from them. Ego Integrity vs. Despair (B) occurs during old age, when people review their lives and feel either satisfaction or regret. Identity vs. Role Confusion (C) occurs during adolescence, when teens either succeed at establishing a personal identity or become confused about what their role is.

73. A: When a parent is widowed or divorced, younger children can be more likely to feel the effects of changes to their usual routines (B) and of the way that their remaining parent copes with the loss (C) than of the death or departure of one parent, rather than vice versa (D). Toddlers may fear losing the other parent as well, so that parent must give them plenty of reassurance and feelings of security.

74. B: Vitamin D is known to help the body absorb the phosphorus and calcium obtained through a person's diet. It is present in small amounts in foods like fish and eggs and is especially present in cod liver oil. Vitamin E is a major antioxidant, meaning that it eliminates cells that can have a deleterious effect on the body. This vitamin is found in good amounts in wheat germ oil, milk, and plant leaves. Vitamin B-3, also known as niacin, helps to reduce levels of cholesterol in the blood. It is found in yeast, dairy products, and wheat germ. Vitamin K promotes blood clotting. It is abundant in spinach, cabbage, and soybeans. Vitamin A contributes to the growth and maintenance of body tissues. It is particularly present in eggs, spinach, and liver.

75. A: Microwave ovens are by far more energy-efficient than the others named, in both cooking efficiency and energy factor. (Cooking efficiency equals the fraction of the total energy the oven consumes that is used to cook food. Energy factor equals the ratio of energy used for cooking food to the total energy consumed.) Convection ovens (B) powered by electricity are more energy-efficient than convection ovens powered by gas; and both kinds of convection ovens are more energy-efficient than traditional electric or gas ovens; but a microwave oven is about 7–8 times more energy-efficient than electric or gas convection ovens, about 5 times more efficient than standard electric ovens, and about 9–10 times more efficient than regular gas ovens. (Note that efficiency refers to energy used, not cost in money, which depends on local rates charged for electricity and gas.)

76. D: A significant portion of American adults consume more sodium (A) than is recommended. This has been associated with an increase in the number of adults who develop hypertension, or high blood pressure, which can threaten an individual's cardiovascular health. Many American adults consume less than the recommended amount of calcium (A), fiber (B), and vitamin D (C). Deficiencies in these nutrients can lead to health complications, but overconsumption of sodium is most closely associated with hypertension.

77. B: Being able to analyze multiple features objectively, evaluate several different plans based on that analysis, and make a decision informed by the evaluation is an example of critical thinking, which is one of the areas whereby the FCCLA helps its members develop life skills. This example does not reflect the area of career preparation (A) because it does not involve learning job skills, identifying career interests, or making career choices. It does not reflect practical knowledge (C) as much as such examples as knowing how to stay within a budget, drive a car, do laundry, cook a meal, etc. It does not reflect interpersonal communication (D) as the student's process of analysis, evaluation, and decision-making did not necessarily involve communicating with other persons.

78. A: Any fat-based dough, e.g., for pie crusts, scones, cookies, or pastries, will become tough if handled too much. When making filled pastries using a buttery (fat-based) pastry dough, pinching the edges together with warm fingers (B) can make the dough too soft rather than tough. (A solution is to chill the dough first and handle it through a piece of plastic wrap.) Overhandling candy clay made with chocolate (C) will make it soften and melt rather than become tough. Putting very wet filling into pie crust (D) will make the dough soggy rather than tough, especially if the pie plate was not buttered or the dough was not brushed with egg white first.

79. B: In the devil's advocacy method, one alternative at a time is presented by the group, and one group member then critiques the alternative and/or the group's process for identifying alternatives by pointing out the drawbacks. In the dialectic inquiry method, two groups each select alternatives and each group then critiques the other group's choices. Managers listen to each group's presentation and critique of alternatives. Thus the number of alternatives presented at a time is one with devil's advocacy and two with dialectic inquiry. With both methods, alternatives are reassessed (A) after being critiqued and/or debated. With both methods, an alternative may be accepted (C). With devil's advocacy, if not accepted the alternative will be rejected or modified; with dialectic inquiry, if both alternatives are not accepted, only one may be accepted; or the two may be combined. With both methods, increasing group diversity has the same effect (D): a broader range of alternatives becomes available with more diverse members contributing.

80. C: These are all true. Historically, curricular deficits developed out of the original separation of academic courses from vocational courses (A), and the parallel separation of students bound for college from students not bound for college (B). Since the implementation of the Common Core Standards, many states now integrate literacy in all vocational and technical subjects with literacy in all academic subjects (D) like language arts, math, science, and social studies.

81. C: The FCCLA's mission to promote students' personal growth and development through Family and Consumer Sciences education aims to help them develop life skills focused on their roles in society as earners of wages (A), members of families (B), and leaders in their communities (D). Although some wage earners, family members, and community leaders are certainly also business owners (C), this is not one of the main roles that the FCCLA specifically focuses on in helping students develop their skills for living.

82. D: The AAFCS states that its leadership works not only to enhance the well-being of individuals, families, and communities (A), but also to influence how consumer goods and services are developed, delivered, and evaluated (B), and to influence both general social change and specific public policymaking (C).

83. B: In Maslow's hierarchy of needs, the bottom of the pyramid represents needs that take priority because they are required for survival. Hence making sure that children get enough food and sleep is ranked by Maslow among his first level, Physiological needs. Maslow's hierarchy is progressive: each needs level must be met before a person can ascend to the next. After meeting physiological needs, the second level is Security needs; for parents this includes ensuring their children have adequate shelter and safety (C). The third level is Social needs; for parents, this includes giving children love, affection, and a sense of belonging (A). The fourth level is Esteem needs; to meet these, parents build high self-esteem and feelings of personal worth (D) in their children. (The fifth level at the top of the pyramid is Self-Actualization Needs, i.e., to fulfill one's fullest potential, after meeting all other needs.)

84. C: If a business owner invests personal cash into the business, the result will be an increase in assets (because cash is an asset account), while liabilities will remain the same and owner's equity will increase because the owner's capital will increase.

85. C: For finding trustworthy online sources of reliable, current health information, the Federal Trade Commission (FTC) recommends visiting federal government agency websites (A), like http://www.nlm.nih.gov/medlineplus/, http://healthfinder.gov/, https://www.healthcare.gov/; http://www.cdc.gov/, http://medicare.gov/, www.fda.gov/consumer, http://www.cancer.gov/, www.nia.nih.gov, and http://womenshealth.gov/. Nonprofit groups focusing on specific diseases or conditions also provide reliable websites (B) offering research information and education to the public; these sites typically have .org extensions (though the FTC also warns consumers to beware phony .org sites set up by scammers). Websites run by medical schools and universities (D)—generally ending with .edu—or by reputable health facilities are also good sources. However, as the FTC points out and many of us have discovered on our own, the results we get from typing any given health topic into a search engine often include unreliable and/or outdated websites.

86. B: Sender-oriented values are characteristic of low-context communication, wherein the speaker is responsible for the clarity of his or her communication, rather than the listeners having responsibility for understanding it (C). This does not mean the speaker ignores the values of the listeners (A). In low-context communication, which has sender-oriented values rather than interpreter-sensitive values (where the listener is responsible to understand), the speaker uses direct patterns of verbal orientation rather than indirect patterns (D), which are used in high-context communication.

87. A: Although the "food pyramid" has long been familiar to most Americans (e.g., the USDA's former MyPyramid and also Mediterranean, Asian, and Latin American Diet Pyramids), the USDA actually replaced MyPyramid with MyPlate in June 2011. Hence the USDA refers to MyPlate as the current government food group symbol rather than MyPyramid (B). MyPlate does not have all of the same food groups as MyPyramid did (C): Whereas MyPyramid contained six food groups, MyPlate has only five because it does not include fats, oils, and sweets as MyPyramid did; hence MyPyramid had more food groups than MyPlate, not fewer (D). (MyPyramid advised "USE SPARINGLY" for this category; due to recent attention to the American obesity epidemic, however, the government decided to eliminate this category altogether as part of a healthful diet.)

88. D: Vitamin C is water-soluble, meaning that it is absorbed into the blood stream and can be forced out of the body through urine and sweat. For example, caffeinated beverages can increase the urine stream and thereby diminish the absorption of water-soluble nutrients like vitamin C. Vitamin B is another water-soluble nutrient. Other vitamins, including A, D, E, and K, are absorbed by the intestinal membrane; these vitamins are said to be fat-soluble. Vitamin D can also be obtained from sunlight.

89. B: The United Nations Guidelines for Consumer Protections (1985) include the right of consumers to a healthy environment. The Consumer Product Safety Commission (A) sets product safety standards, as do the Underwriters' Laboratories (C). The Bureau of Competition (D) protects investors who purchase tradable financial assets like bonds, stocks, etc., and helps provide that a wide selection of goods and services is available to consumers.

90. D: Problem-solving skills are among the critical thinking skills needed not only for academic activities, but also in real life including household management. Consumer and family sciences teach these. The first thing necessary to solve a problem is to identify what the problem is. Identifying different actions that could be taken (A); predicting what the results of those actions might be (B); and collecting information related to the problem (C) depend on, and cannot be done without, first defining the specific problem to be solved.

91. B: It is recommended that 20 to 35 percent of total calorie consumption should be from fats; 45 to 65 percent of total calories should be carbohydrates; and 10 to 35 percent should be protein.

92. C: One component of CBT is breaking linkages or associations between eating/food and other things when those connections contribute to overeating, emotional eating, poor food choices, etc. Some techniques for breaking linkages include not eating in certain environments; not keeping poor food choices at home; finding alternatives to eating as coping mechanisms; obtaining social support; changing eating habits; using positive reinforcement, problem-solving strategies, rehearsal, etc. Another component of CBT involves positive self-statements (A), used to replace self-defeating thoughts (e.g., "I'll never change," "This is too difficult," etc.). Evaluating readiness for change (B) is a component of CBT wherein the individual becomes aware of what s/he needs to do to attain his/her weight management goals, and then commits to doing those things. Self-monitoring (D) is a component of CBT wherein one keeps track of things like food choices, portion sizes, and factors other than hunger that trigger eating. This increases eating self-awareness and supports focusing on long-term success.

93. C: The automobile manufacturer failed to meet consumer rights regarding liability. If any of the engines catch fire, the manufacturer is liable for any injuries resulting from the fire and also any damage to the vehicle. Consumers have the right to rely on the products they purchase to meet minimum safety standards.

94. C: "Demonstrate measuring, estimating, ordering, purchasing, pricing, and repurposing skills" is Competency 11.3.3 of Content Standard 11.3. "Critique design plans to address client's needs, goals, and resources" (A) is Competency 11.6.4 of Content Standard 11.6: "Evaluate client's needs, goals, and resources in creating design plans for housing and residential and commercial interiors." "Describe features of furnishings that are characteristic of various historical periods" (B) is Competency 11.5.1 of Content Standard 11.5: "Analyze design and development of architecture, interiors, and furnishings through the ages." "Demonstrate procedures for reporting and handling accidents, safety, and security incidents" (D) is Competency 11.8.4 of Content Standard 11.8: "Analyze professional practices, procedures for business profitability and career success, and the role of ethics in the housing, interiors and furnishings industries."

95. B: Free cash flow calculates how much cash a business generates after accounting for capital expenditures such as buildings or equipment. This cash can be used for expansion, dividends, reducing debt, or other purposes. To calculate free cash flow, the following equation is used: free cash flow = net income + non-cash expenses – increase in working capital – capital expenditures. Calculating free cash flow requires multiple steps but is one of the most useful calculations that a business owner can make to determine the financial health of a business. An enterprise budget is an estimate of the costs and returns to produce a product. Although this would be helpful to her, she needs to determine if the business can afford to expand first. Net income explains how much the business sold but does not take into account any debts and therefore can be misleading. Capital expenditure calculates the money a business spends on purchasing or maintaining a fixed asset, such as land or the business building.

96. C: The best option for funding the new printer is likely crowdfunding. If Stan can convince enough individual lenders to support his cause, he can raise the needed capital. The bank would likely decline his request for a loan because the business has not demonstrated the ability to earn enough revenue to prove worthy of lending. Venture capitalists generally invest in more mature and stable companies. Stan is barely breaking even each year, so it is not likely he will be able to fund the cost of the printer with his own cash (bootstrapping).

97. D: Palm oil is not an unsaturated fat. On the contrary, it is a saturated fat, meaning that excessive consumption of it can lead to heart disease. Coconut oil, butter, and lard are some of the other saturated fats. The other answer choices are unsaturated fats, which are better for the body. In fact, olive oil and canola oil can reduce the amount of cholesterol in the body.

98. B: Food manufacturers now add folic acid to their products because it has been shown to reduce the risk of spinal bifida in infants. Folic acid is a B vitamin that aids in the synthesis of hemoglobin, which is required to transport oxygen throughout the bloodstream. Pregnant women, women who are trying to become pregnant, and elderly people should all ensure that their diet includes foods with folic acid. There are also a number of safe supplements containing folic acid.

99. D: The major benefit of vitamin A is that it helps the body produce healthy hair and skin. Carrots, pumpkins, fish, and eggs are all good sources of vitamin A. Help with forming new cells is a major benefit of folate, or folic acid. There is a great deal of folate in spinach and fortified grains. Vitamin C is one of the primary disease-fighting nutrients. It is obtained most effectively from citrus fruits and broccoli. Concentration and alertness are improved by vitamin B-12. It is most abundant in fish, poultry, and eggs. Calcium is a mineral that helps muscles contract. It is abundant in dairy products and sardines.

100. C: The realtor should regularly update information s/he gives the consumer about the conditions of the current housing market (A), available financing options (B), and situation-specific negotiating tactics (D). Buying a house can be a lengthy process, and market conditions can change, sometimes in relatively short periods. So can financing options: lenders can offer new products; different providers may offer different financing plans, and the realtor can recommend some that may suit the consumer better than others; the buyer's credit score and financial resources can change, etc. Also, some strategies for negotiating can apply to some situations, but not others wherein different techniques are more appropriate.

101. C: The principle of not exploiting people is under the Conflict of Interest category of the AAFCS Principles of Professional Practice in its Code of Ethics. The Professional Competence (A) category includes principles related to credentials; professional development; education, training, experience; claims of competence; and practice within legal limits. The Respect for Diversity (B) category pertains to practices that support diversity and respecting differences in cultural beliefs and backgrounds. The Confidentiality (D) category covers trust, respect, cooperation and confidentiality, and protecting people's confidential information in professional relationships.

102. A: Both sisters were involved in promoting the domestic sciences prior to the birth of the home economics movement with the first of the Lake Placid Conferences in 1899. Catherine Beecher (B) was an educator, and her sister Harriet Beecher Stowe (C), an abolitionist known for authoring *Uncle Tom's Cabin.* They were both champions of women's education and early leaders in the foundations of home economics/family and consumer sciences. Therefore, that neither of them did this (D) is incorrect.

103. B: Children in the early school years, e.g., from four to six years old, have developmental tasks including learning to play in groups, identifying with a gender role, and early moral development. Toddlers (A), e.g., from two to four years old, have developmental tasks including locomotion beyond toddling; symbolic representation and pretend play; developing language; and learning self-control. Children in middle school (C), e.g., from six to twelve years old, have developmental tasks including making friends; performing concrete mental operations; learning academic and social skills; participating as a team member in playing games; and evaluating themselves. Infants (A), e.g., from birth to two years old, have developmental tasks including motor, perceptual, and sensory maturation; basic emotional development; social attachment; sensorimotor cognition; understanding basic causation, objects, and categorizing.

104. C: "Analyze physical, emotional, social, spiritual, and intellectual development" is Competency 12.1.1 of Content Standard 12.1. "Analyze the effect of heredity and environment on human growth and development" (A) is Competency 12.2.1 under Content Standard 12.2: "Analyze conditions that influence human growth and development." "Analyze the effects of gender, ethnicity, and culture on individual development" (B) is Competency 12.2.3, also under Content Standard 12.2 (above). D. "Analyze the role of communication on human growth and development" (D) is Competency 12.3.2 under Content Standard 12.3: "Analyze strategies that promote growth and development across the life span."

105. A: Within the wide range of specialties available in FCS education, financial planning is one that is currently needed by many financial institutions. This includes brokerage firms; banks and savings and loan associations, which *are* also looking for financial planners (B); and insurance companies and also counseling agencies (C). Qualified financial planners *do* need to understand both the relationship with community and also family dynamics (D) to serve these financial institutions best.

106. C: The AAFCS' Healthy Weight Resolution was issued in 2011 to support national nutrition education and obesity prevention. The AAFCS made a resolution that a class in Life and Career Choices should be required in middle schools and junior high schools (A) in 2007. The AAFCS issued a resolution supporting education and policies that promoting health literacy (B) in 2010. The AAFCS resolved in 2003 that the 10th anniversary of the United Nations International Year of the Family should be observed (D) in 2004.

107. C: Quilting is the fabrication method of stitching a liner fabric in between two outer fabrics. Because this process essentially creates a three-layered fabric, it is used in outerwear and clothing that is meant for cold weather. Knitting is the use of hooked needles to loop yarn threads together. Fabrics made by knitting tend to be very flexible. In stitch-through, a web of fiber is stitched together by a chain of smaller stitches. This technique is also known as malimo. Tufting is a process in which a woven backing has yarns inserted into it, where they are sealed in place with glue. This process, commonly used in the manufacture of carpets, is occasionally used in apparel as well. Finally, weaving is the creation of a network of three yarns, interconnected at right angles throughout the fabric.

108. C: In his theory, Maslow proposed a progressive hierarchy of needs, often illustrated in a pyramid: He proposed each level of needs must be met before any higher level(s). The most basic needs essential to survival, which must be met first, are at the pyramid's base/bottom. Maslow termed these physiological needs, e.g., food, water, and sleep. As these come before all others, (A) is incorrect. At the pyramid's point/tip/top, Maslow placed "self-actualizing needs," i.e., to fulfill one's highest potentials. These can only be realized after all other needs lower on the pyramid are met; hence (B) is incorrect. Maslow placed "security needs," i.e., for shelter and safety, second after physiological needs (C). Needing to feel love, affection, and belonging, i.e., what Maslow called "social needs" are third in his hierarchy; what he termed "esteem needs," i.e., to have self-esteem and feel personal worth, social recognition, and accomplishment are fourth. Hence (D) is incorrect.

109. A: Legumes, that is, beans, split peas, and lentils, are classified in both the vegetables and the proteins food groups by the US Department of Agriculture (cf. ChooseMyPlate.gov) because they have much higher protein content than other vegetables. Seafood (B) is in the protein food group only. Cheese (C) is in the dairy food group only. Eggplant (D) is in the vegetable food group only.

110. B: All of these accurately describe women's nutritional requirements. Women differ from men not only in numbers of calories, but also in the amounts they need of various nutrients. And even among women alone, their nutritional needs will not be the same at different times during their menstrual cycles (C), or when they are pregnant, or when they are breastfeeding (nursing) infants (D).

111. B: Early childhood is a period of rapid bone growth, so young children need more calcium in their diets than older children or adults (except pregnant women, nursing mothers, menopausal/post-menopausal women, and elderly adults, who also need more calcium and vitamin D). Nutritionists recommend serving young children 2-3 daily servings of dairy products and/or other foods high in calcium. Young children need adequate levels of magnesium (A) and potassium (C), but not extra amounts as of calcium for bone support. They do not need extra starches (D), and those they do eat should be whole-grain rather than refined flours.

112. A: Interpreter-sensitive values are characteristic of high-context communication and mean the listener is expected to take responsibility for interpreting the speaker's meaning, much of which is conveyed through nonverbal behaviors (C), which the listener must "read between the lines" (D) to infer. Conversely, low-context communication uses sender-oriented values, meaning the speaker is expected to take responsibility for communicating clearly and directly (B) to make decoding simple (D) for the listener.

113. D: Of the given fabrics, black satin would offer the best protection against sunlight. Dark clothing tends to protect the body from ultraviolet radiation better, because they absorb rather than reflect the rays of the sun. Moreover, densely woven fabrics like satin have fewer holes through which sunlight can flow. Of course, black satin might not be the most comfortable fabric to wear in the sun. Dark clothing gets very hot, and sweating in satin clothing can be unpleasant. Many people prefer to wear cotton clothing, because the looser weave allows for superior ventilation. However, cotton offers little protection against UV rays, so it is important to wear sunscreen under the clothing.

114. B: Making ethically sound decisions is a principle under the Integrity heading of the AAFCS Code of Ethics Principles of Conduct. Protecting private information (A) is a principle under the Confidentiality heading of these principles. Practicing within the limits of one's expertise (C) is a principle under the Professional Competence heading. Treating consumers, as well as colleagues, individuals, and families, with fairness (D) and avoiding divided loyalties is a principle under the Conflict of Interest heading.

115. C: The food and appliance industry currently is seeing increases in the number of jobs available for FCS professionals. The rapidity of social change today increases individual stress throughout the life span; this increases the need for human services administration rather than reducing it (A). Health care jobs, especially long-term care administration, wellness, and dependent care, are not remaining stable (B) but are increasing. Employment opportunities in the hospitality industries, i.e., hotels, motels, and restaurants, and travel and tourism industries are not currently decreasing (D), but expanding as well.

116. A: Losing weight quickly decreases the metabolism. Nutritionists and doctors believe that this is a form of self-defense by the body, which senses that food is not as available and therefore tries to limit its use of calories. All of the other answer choices are events that increase metabolism. Weight gain always raises metabolism, in part because there is more muscle or fat to provide with nutrients. Muscle burns more calories than fat, so an increase in muscle mass will correlate with an increase in metabolism. Any exercise tends to increase metabolism.

117. B: This is defined as an extended family because a grandparent lives with the parents and children. A nuclear family (A) is defined as only the parents and children living together. A blended family (C) is formed when two parents, each with children from a previous marriage or relationship, marry each other and both sets of children live together with both parents. A combined family (D) is not a commonly used term, but may be used as a synonym for a blended family.

118. B: In a dumbbell layout pattern, spaces are arranged along a linear path, with major elements at either end. This layout pattern is appropriate for houses or buildings in which there are two main places of activity, and it is a good idea to keep the areas separate. A radial layout consists of a number of paths extending out from a central point. This kind of arrangement is typical of offices and buildings with one central purpose. In a clustered layout, several spaces with similar size, shape, and function are grouped close together and linked along a central space or corridor. A doughnut layout, as exemplified by the Pentagon, consists of a circular corridor with rooms on either side. A centralized layout consists of secondary elements arranged around a central point, or axis. One example of a centralized layout is a plaza, in which the central point may be a statue or fountain.

119. A: Borrowers with a poor credit rating will not be eligible for a bank's prime rate. The prime rate is the lowest rate of interest offered by a commercial bank or other lending institution. It is made available only to borrowers with pristine credit ratings, since these people and businesses are most likely to repay the loan according to the agreed-upon schedule. Savings deposits, demand deposits, and certificates of deposit are all investitures made by the consumer in a bank, and therefore do not depend on credit rating. A savings deposit can be withdrawn at any time, while a certificate of deposit must be kept in the bank for a prescribed length of time. A demand deposit is essentially the same thing as a checking account, because the funds within it can be withdrawn at any time and in any amount. Banks are required to have deposit insurance to guarantee that they will be able to return the funds invested by customers.

120. D: Having access to information that supports better purchasing decisions is an example of the consumer's right to education. Minimizing environmental impacts through purchasing choices (A) is an example of a consumer's *responsibility* to promote a healthy environment. An example of the consumer's *right* to a healthy environment is to reside and work in environments that are not detrimental to the consumer's health. Following safety instruction to ensure the safe use of products (B) is an example of a consumer's *responsibility* for safety. An example of a consumer's *right* to safety is to be protected against health hazards in products and services. Sustainable consumption that will not impinge on others' needs (C) is an example of a consumer's *responsibility* to meet basic needs. An example of a consumer's *right* to have basic needs met is to have access to shelter, water, and food.

Practice Test #2

1. Research has found which of the following most often?

a. Parents are more likely to expect more of their youngest children.
b. Parents are more likely to expect more from their middle children.
c. Parents are more likely to expect the same from all their children.
d. Parents are more likely to expect more of their firstborn children.

2. The child who assumes the role of the family artist, rebel, peacemaker, troublemaker, clown, or negotiator is most often which child in birth order?

a. The firstborn child
b. The middle child
c. The second child
d. The only child

3. The Family and Medical Leave Act of 1993 requires employers to give eligible employees unpaid time off with job protection. Which of these *most* accurately identifies the reasons allowed for this leave?

a. Maternity leave exclusively.
b. Maternity *or* paternity leave.
c. Maternity *and* paternity leave.
d. Family and/or medical reasons.

4. When children become part of a remarried family with other children, which of these is true?

a. A child's rank in the family never changes.
b. The role each child plays remains distinct.
c. All these factors are most likely to change.
d. Incest taboos are the same for all siblings.

5. According to Evelyn Duvall's description of the Family Life Cycle, which of these accurately represents two consecutive stages of the family life cycle?

a. Married couples without children; families with children from birth to 6 years
b. Families with children from birth to 6 years; families with children 6-13 years
c. Families with children 0–30 months; families with children 24 months-6 years
d. Families with teen children 13–20 years; "empty nest" couples to retirement

6. In some models of family life stages, which task is most typical of the "later family life" stage?

a. Helping children develop peer relationships
b. Assuming the care for one's family of origin
c. Reminiscing and integrating life experiences
d. Coping with deaths in one's family of origin

7. Which of these correctly relates a stage in each theory to the same age periods and family stages?

a. Freud's Oedipal; Erikson's Autonomy vs. Shame, Doubt; Piaget's Preoperational; Duvall's School Age
b. Freud's Anal; Erikson's Industry vs. Inferiority; Piaget's Formal Operations; Duvall's with Preschoolers
c. Freud's Genital; Erikson's Initiative vs. Guilt; Piaget's Concrete Operations; Duvall's with Teenagers
d. Freud's Oral; Erikson's Basic Trust vs. Mistrust; Piaget's Sensorimotor; Duvall's Families with Infants

8. Freud's Latency stage corresponds most closely in terms of child development with

a. Kohlberg's Pre-Conventional stage in his theory of moral development.
b. Erikson's psychosocial development stage, Identity vs. Role Confusion.
c. Piaget's stage of cognitive development he termed Formal Operations.
d. Duvall's Families with School-Age Children stage of family development.

9. Erikson's psychosocial developmental stage of Ego Integrity vs. Despair corresponds to which of Duvall's stages of family development?

a. Stage VIII: Aging Families
b. Stage VII: Middle-Aged Families
c. Stage VI: Families as Launching Centers
d. Stage IV: Families with School-Age Children

10. According to the attachment styles defined by Mary Ainsworth through her Strange Situation experiments, which of these did she observe about separation anxiety in children aged 12–18 months?

a. Children who have secure attachments show distress when their mothers leave the room.
b. Children with insecure-ambivalent attachment show no distress if mother leaves the room.
c. Children with insecure-avoidant attachment show extreme distress at the mother's leaving.
d. Children with secure attachment show higher separation anxiety than insecure-ambivalent.

11. According to Diana Baumrind's theory of parenting styles, which style is considered the ideal?

a. Permissive
b. Authoritarian
c. Authoritative
d. Uninvolved

12. Baumrind and other researchers applying her theory of parenting styles have found that children who function at low levels in multiple areas of life are most likely to have had parents with which style?

a. Permissive
b. Authoritarian
c. Uninvolved
d. Authoritative

13. According to Schaefer's model of parenting along continua across two dimensions, which of these most accurately corresponds with Baumrind's subsequent definition of parenting styles?

a. Parents high in warmth/low in hostility and high in control/low in autonomy have a permissive style.
b. Parents high in hostility/low in warmth and high in autonomy/low in control have authoritarian style.
c. Parents high in autonomy/low in control and high in hostility/low in warmth have an uninvolved style.
d. Parents high in warmth/low in hostility and high in autonomy/low in control have authoritative style.

14. According to Bandura's Social Learning Theory, four conditions are needed for modeling of behaviors to occur. Which of these is most related to having a good reason to imitate another's behavior?

a. Attention
b. Motivation
c. Retention
d. Reproduction

15. Which of the following more accurately reflects what Bandura believed in developing his social learning theory?

a. The environment an individual is in causes his or her behavior.
b. Environment, behavior, and psychological processes interact.
c. The behavior of an individual creates his or her environment.
d. Psychological processes cause the environment and behavior.

16. Regarding needs parents must meet for children, which of the following is correct according to the hierarchy of needs Abraham Maslow proposed in his humanistic theory of motivation and personality?

a. Parents must make children feel they are loved before worrying about their feeding and rest.
b. Enabling children to fulfill their highest potentials in life takes precedence over all other needs.
c. Before they can keep children safe, parents must see they get enough water, food, and sleep.
d. Parents should promote children's self-esteem first and then their family acceptance and love.

17. When a couple with children divorces, which family relationship factors often receive direct and/or indirect effects?

a. The structure of the family
b. The income for the family
c. Community expectations
d. All these can be affected

18. A variety of researchers have found evidence that family recreation provides many benefits, both to families and to individual family members. Which of the following is an example of one of family recreation's benefits to the family as a group?

a. Teaching moral values and health
b. Improvements in communications
c. Providing educational experiences
d. Fulfilling a diversity among needs

19. In which of Erikson's stages of development do individuals measure their success by what they contribute to their families and society?

a. Intimacy vs. Isolation
b. Ego Integrity vs. Despair
c. Identity vs. Role Confusion
d. Generativity vs. Stagnation

20. In describing stages of child development, which ages did Arnold Gesell characterize as periods of equilibrium, consolidation, and smoothness?

a. 2½, 5½ to 6, and 11 years
b. 2, 5, 10, and 16 years
c. 3½, 7, and 13 years
d. 4, 8, and 14 years

21. In the developmental tasks he identified for different age groups across the life span, which of the following did Robert Havighurst include as a task during middle age?

a. Adopting civic responsibilities
b. Adjusting to physical changes
c. Meeting social/civic obligation
d. Socially responsible behaviors

22. When describing moral development, Piaget characterized two types of adult-child relationships. In the _____ relationship, the adult _____ the child; in the ______ relation, the adult _____ the child.

a. Heteronomous, "co-operates" with; autonomous, coerces
b. Unilateral, respects; reciprocal, controls and/or constrains
c. Interactive, constrains; heteronomous, "co-operates" with
d. Heteronomous, coerces; autonomous, "co-operates" with

23. According to psychologists, the level of Safety needs in Maslow's hierarchy would typically be a priority for which developmental period?

a. Infancy
b. Adulthood
c. Adolescence
d. Toddlerhood

24. A child whose developmental tasks include learning to play in groups, to identify as a female or male, and to have a basic understanding of right and wrong is typically in which life stage?

a. The toddler years
b. Early school years
c. Middle school age
d. Birth to two years

25. During which life stage is it most typical to focus on developmental tasks like thinking abstractly, attaining peer group membership, and experiencing sexual relationships?

a. Early adolescence
b. Later adolescence
c. Middle school age
d. In early adulthood

26. According to models of developmental tasks at various life stages, when is an adult most likely to develop a perspective related to death?

a. Around age 22–34
b. Around age 34–60
c. Around age 60–75
d. Around 75–death

27. Which special needs are most often characteristic in autism spectrum disorders?

a. Difficulty focusing and maintaining attention
b. Difficulty understanding and using social cues
c. Difficulty with motor control and coordination
d. Difficulty with adhering to consistent routines

28. Which special resource(s) would most likely be needed by someone with spina bifida?

a. A communication board
b. Text-to-speech software
c. A wheelchair or crutches
d. Cochlear implantation(s)

29. The impact on a child's development of local and global communities belongs in which of the systems in Bronfenbrenner's ecological systems theory?

a. The chronosystem
b. The microsystem
c. The mesosystem
d. The exosystem

30. Whereas Freud focused on male development in proposing the concept of the Oedipal conflict, neo-Freudians expanded on his theory to include the Elektra conflict for girls. In the latter, what must a girl do to resolve this conflict and thereafter have successful interpersonal relationships?

a. Nothing; they just grow out of it
b. Symbolically "kill" their mothers
c. Want to be just like their fathers
d. Want to be just like the mothers

31. The research of Walter Toman (also adopted by Murray Bowen) found that in the workplace, which relationship is likely to be most harmonious and effective?

a. A boss and an assistant who were both oldest children working together
b. A boss and assistant who were both youngest children working together
c. A boss who was an oldest child and an assistant who was a youngest child
d. A boss who was a youngest child and an assistant who was an oldest child

32. Family therapist Virginia Satir identified five common roles of family members. She described only Levelers, who communicate their true feelings honestly, as healthy because their outward communication is congruent with their inward emotions. Which of the other four dysfunctional roles hopes to be loved by being perceived as harmlessly endearing?

a. Blamers
b. Placators
c. Distractors
d. Computers

33. In describing high-context vs. low-context styles of communication, what do "sender-oriented values" mean?

a. The speakers do not consider the values of the listeners.
b. The speaker has responsibility for clearly communicating.
c. The speaker lets listeners be responsible to understand.
d. The speaker uses indirect patterns of verbal orientation.

34. Which of the following is true about one channel of nonverbal communication?

a. Eye contact while speaking is one culturally dependent orientation.
b. Eye contact while speaking is treated universally across all cultures.
c. Eye contact while speaking is preferred in Japan as long and direct.
d. Eye contact while speaking is direct for all USA audience members.

35. Regarding nonverbal forms of communicating, which statement is most accurate?

a. Messages conveyed via nonverbal means are not found as truthful as verbal messages are.
b. The use of humor in speaking is not included among the areas of nonverbal communication.
c. Increasing globalization means that nonverbal communication is more universally the same.
d. Increasing globalization requires more awareness, observation, and sensitivity of speakers.

36. When giving advice, which example is the recipient most likely to hear instead of perceiving it as unsolicited, unwanted, and coercive?

a. "You may find that easier to do if you try doing this."
b. "You must do it this way or it's never going to work."
c. "There is only one way to do that right and this is it."
d. "That's not working because you're doing it wrong."

37. Among the following developmental theories, what is correct relative to development across the life span?

a. Freud and Piaget had theories that cover the life span, while Erikson's ends at adolescence.
b. Piaget's and Erikson's theories do not go beyond adolescence while Freud's goes to death.
c. Freud's and Erikson's theories cover all of life while Piaget's theory stops with adolescence.
d. Erikson's theory has developmental stages across the life span; Freud's and Piaget's do not.

38. Among the following, which is an example of a consumer right?

a. Minimizing environmental impacts through purchasing choices
b. Following safety instructions to ensure the safe use of products
c. Sustainable consumption that will not impinge on others' needs
d. Accessing information that supports better purchasing decisions

39. Which provision of the Wall Street Reform and Consumer Protection Act of 2009 fulfills the consumer rights and responsibilities regarding redress?

a. Brokers have advisors' duties if advising on investments.
b. Advisors must give information to the SEC upon request.
c. Whistleblowers who disclose wrongdoing are protected.
d. Consumers can sue credit rating agencies for negligence.

40. When was the Federal Trade Commission (FTC) established?

a. 1914
b. 1934
c. 1979
d. 1995

41. One factor that influences consumers to consider prices more in their health care decisions is:

a. When they have no prior ideas of provider quality.
b. When their health insurance plan is a PPO or HMO.
c. When they have a severe and/or urgent condition.
d. When they have health care practitioners they like.

42. When using product or service information to inform consumer decisions, which of these is an example of "soft" information?

a. Weight
b. Pricing
c. Quality
d. Content

43. In determining one's current financial situation for financial planning, what is true about which elements to include?

a. For planning purposes, use total income after taxes.
b. Living expenses and debts are really the same thing.
c. When listing assets, including savings is unnecessary.
d. When listing income, use gross income before taxes.

44. Which of these is most realistic about analyzing financial values and developing financial goals?

a. Other people cannot recommend any financial goals for an individual.
b. Other people should advise an individual of goals and which to pursue.
c. Individuals must decide for themselves which financial goals to pursue.
d. Financial goals should include saving and investing but never spending.

45. What is true about information on clothing labels, tags, or packages?

a. Manufacturers are required by law to provide only registered ID number identification.
b. Manufacturers are required by law to show ID, fiber content, country, and care instructions.
c. Manufacturers are required by law to indicate only the country where clothing is made.
d. Manufacturers are required by law to show fiber content; care instructions are optional.

46. What information is required by law for Nutrition Facts panels on food packaging to include?

a. Serving size, number of servings, and calories per serving
b. Amounts of protein, carbohydrates, and fats per serving
c. Fiber, sodium, vitamins, and minerals are not necessary.
d. All of these and more information are required by law.

47. In the Nutrition Facts panels on food packages, how is the amount of calcium represented?

a. The number of milligrams
b. In number of micrograms
c. As percent of serving size
d. As percent of Daily Value

48. Among the following cognitive biases to which management is subject, which one is caused by making a decision based on an incorrect generalization from an isolated instance or a sample that is too small?

a. Prior hypothesis bias
b. Illusion of control bias
c. Representativeness bias
d. Escalating commitment bias

49. As two separate ways of improving decision-making in management, what is a major difference between devil's advocacy and dialectic inquiry?

a. Alternative reassessments
b. The number of alternatives
c. Acceptance of alternatives
d. Effects of greater diversity

50. Relative to prioritization for time management, what does the "80/20 Rule" mean?

a. 80% of the people in any workplace contribute 20% of the effort.
b. 80% of what we do contributes less than 20% to our work's value.
c. The formula for work success is 80% perspiration, 20% inspiration.
d. In typical workplaces, 80% of time is well used and 20% is wasted.

51. In researching elder-care services online, which website helps consumers find their local Area Agency on Aging (AAA)?

a. Medicare website: http://medicare.gov/
b. LeadingAge (IAHSA) website: http://www.leadingage.org/
c. Eldercare.gov website: http://eldercare.gov/
d. Assisted Living Federation website: http://www.alfa.org/alfa/

52. When working parents look for services to care for their children, which of these is accurate?

a. Because of recent economic factors, many caregivers are charging higher rates.
b. Grandparent child care is less common with fewer extended families cohabiting.
c. To be competitive, "hybrid" providers offer parents additional services included.
d. Au pairs' wages are a bigger challenge than associated government regulations.

53. Which of the following websites is *best* for finding energy-efficient home appliances at no charge?

a. www.sears.com/
b. http://products.construction.com/
c. www.consumerreports.org
d. www.energystar.gov

54. Safety is a primary consideration in choosing toys for children. Experts also advise choosing toys from which children can learn; that keep their attention more than briefly; that do not promote aggression; and that parents will also enjoy playing with and will not find irritating. What else is recommended in choosing toys?

a. Parents should choose different toys for girls than toys they pick for boys.
b. Social interaction and creativity are equally important for toys to promote.
c. Toys that stimulate one sense at a time rather than several are preferable.
d. Problem-solving supersedes eye-hand coordination in what toys develop.

55. The nutritional requirements of women:

a. Differ from the requirements of men.
b. Are accurately described by all these.
c. Vary throughout the menstrual cycle.
d. Differ when pregnant and/or nursing.

56. Which of the following nutrients is commonly associated with an increased risk of hypertension?

a. Calcium
b. Fiber
c. Vitamin D
d. Sodium

57. Vegetarians can get non-heme iron from plant sources, but to improve absorption of these, they should eat them together with foods rich in:

a. Calcium.
b. Vitamin C.
c. Vitamin D.
d. Vitamin E.

58. Which of these dairy foods has the most calcium?

a. A 4.2-oz. slice of fruit cheesecake
b. A 5.3-oz. serving of low-fat yogurt
c. A 1.4-oz. chunk of cheddar cheese
d. A 2.6-oz. serving of plain ice cream

59. Which of these vitamins build up to harmful levels in the body if too much are ingested?

a. Vitamins C and D
b. Vitamins A, D, E, K
c. Vitamin B complex
d. Vitamins never do

60. The USDA recommends that in a healthy diet, at least half of the plate should be:

a. Proteins, with grains.
b. Vegetables and dairy.
c. Grains and dairy food.
d. Fruits and vegetables.

61. Which of these is true about the %DV (Daily Value) the FDA requires on food labels?

a. They make it easier for consumers to know in numbers how much they need of nutrients in a day.
b. They make it easier for consumers to know how much of a day's allowance of nutrients a food has.
c. They make it harder for consumers to comparison shop for foods by the relative nutrient amounts.
d. They were developed by the FDA to replace RDAs because the RDAs were found to be inaccurate.

62. Which of the following disorders *always* involves bingeing and purging by definition?

a. Neither one
b. Anorexia
c. Bulimia
d. Both

63. Which is *most* accurate today about type 1 and type 2 diabetes?

a. Type 1 diabetes is only inherited, while type 2 diabetes only develops from lifestyle.
b. Type 1 diabetes is from lack of insulin; type 2 diabetes is from insensitivity to insulin.
c. Type 1 diabetes occurs in childhood, while type 2 diabetes occurs during adulthood.
d. Type 1 diabetes accounts for half of all cases and type 2 diabetes for the other half.

64. Which of the following is most consistent with expert advice for healthy eating?

a. Tracking eating patterns causes obsession and compulsion.
b. Exercising is a superior antidote for boredom than eating is.
c. An effective way to decrease food intake is skipping meals.
d. Certain foods that are not healthful should never be eaten.

65. When used for weight management, which component of cognitive-behavioral therapy (CBT) is most reflected in a person's not eating in certain environments?

a. Positive self-statements
b. Readiness for change
c. Breaking linkages
d. Self-monitoring

66. When planning a menu, which should be decided upon first?

a. What the entrée of the meal will be
b. What side dishes of the meal will be
c. What the décor for the meal will be
d. What to prepare with foods bought

67. Which of these reflects proper dining etiquette when attending dinner parties?

a. When passing dishes, they should be passed clockwise.
b. Bread only should be passed around the table clockwise.
c. Guests should pass all dishes including bread to the right.
d. It is up to the individual guests whether to cut up foods.

68. Among these food preparation factors, which can cause food poisoning or other food-borne illness?

a. All of these can cause it with certain foods.
b. Cooking foods for the wrong lengths of time
c. Cooking foods at the wrong temperatures
d. Not pasteurizing or refrigerating some foods

69. Which of these cooking methods is the most energy-efficient?

a. A microwave oven
b. A convection oven
c. An electric oven
d. A gas oven

70. Of the following types of fat, which is considered the *most* harmful?

a. Partially hydrogenated vegetable oil
b. Fully hydrogenated vegetable oil
c. Monounsaturated fat
d. Polyunsaturated fat

71. Which of the following is *most* accurate regarding freeze-dried cheese?

a. Freeze-dried cheese costs more than fresh cheese does.
b. Freeze-dried cheese is less expensive than fresh cheese.
c. Experts advise replacing fresh cheeses with freeze-dried.
d. No reconstituting method makes it just like fresh cheese.

72. What do wardrobe experts advise to individuals for cleaning out their closets?

a. To get rid of anything they have not worn in more than a year
b. To get rid of anything that does not fit them and keep the rest
c. To get rid of anything and everything meeting all these criteria
d. To get rid of anything that is not suited to their personal styles

73. When reorganizing clothes, which is the best advice regarding clothing colors?

a. We should discard any items in colors outside of our most flattering color group.
b. We should keep a few items in colors outside our color group to ensure variety.
c. We should coordinate all the colors of our clothes for maximum outfit potential.
d. We should do (A) and (C) to look our best and make creating outfits the easiest.

74. Some color analysts divide people's coloring into the four seasons for choosing the most flattering palette of colors in clothing and makeup. Others use adjectives associated with temperaments for the same purpose. Which of the following correctly equates these two systems?

a. "Passionate" = "Autumn"; "Dramatic" = "Winter"; "Vibrant" = "Spring"; "Romantic" = "Summer"
b. "Dramatic" = "Autumn"; "Passionate" = "Winter"; "Romantic" = "Spring"; "Vibrant" = "Summer"
c. "Vibrant" = "Autumn"; "Romantic" = "Winter"; "Passionate" = "Spring"; "Dramatic" = "Summer"
d. "Romantic" = "Autumn"; "Vibrant" = "Winter"; "Dramatic" = "Spring"; "Passionate" = "Summer"

75. Of the following, which is generally the most flattering cut and line to wear for a woman with full hips and thin legs?

a. A circle skirt
b. A pencil skirt
c. A fishtail skirt
d. An A-line skirt

76. In fabric that is woven using a triaxial weave, what is the third set of yarn called?

a. The warp
b. The weft
c. The whug
d. The woof

77. In the process of finishing knitted or woven fabrics, which of these reflects the correct sequence?

a. Bleaching or brightening, cleaning, dyeing, singeing, Mercerizing
b. Cleaning, singeing, bleaching or brightening, Mercerizing, dyeing
c. Mercerizing, bleaching or brightening, dyeing, cleaning, singeing
d. Bleaching or brightening, dyeing, Mercerizing, singeing, cleaning

78. Which of the following fabric care symbols indicates a garment should be line-dried or hang-dried?

a. A square with diagonal lines in a corner
b. A square with one horizontal line inside
c. A square with three vertical lines inside
d. A square with a horizontal arc at the top

79. Which of the following is true about purchasing a home, according to realtors?

a. To buy a house with a mortgage, some down payment is always necessary.
b. When purchasing a home, the buyer is always responsible for closing costs.
c. Some loan programs give buyers no money down and few/no closing costs.
d. Monthly mortgage payments are not affected by the down payment made.

80. Which of these is most accurate about realtors who help consumers buy homes?

a. Some realtors represent buyers, while others represent sellers.
b. All practicing realtors represent both the buyers and the sellers.
c. Some realtors represent buyers or sellers, while others do both.
d. Whether realtors represent buyers or sellers varies individually.

81. Why do realtors usually advise consumers to obtain pre-approval before choosing a home to buy?

a. To determine how much money they can afford to spend
b. To be able to accomplish all of these through pre-approval
c. To identify which loan programs will meet their needs best
d. To allow time to find lenders and have their credit checked

82. In the realty market, in most US states a "first-time buyer" means:

a. Anyone who has never owned real estate property before.
b. Anyone who has only owned property less than six months.
c. Anyone who has not owned property in the last three years.
d. Anyone who did own, but does not currently own, property.

83. Where can a consumer obtain a mortgage loan to buy a house?

a. Consumers can acquire loans from any and all of these sources today.
b. Mortgage bankers or mortgage brokers are the only sources for loans.
c. Savings and loans, credit unions, various banks, or insurance companies
d. Increasing numbers of realtors can arrange mortgage financing today.

84. When should a home buyer get warranty and insurance coverage for the home?

a. After closing before moving in
b. When making a bid on a house
c. At the closing of the home sale
d. When applying for a mortgage

85. Regarding the essential human right to housing, which of the following UN events took place the earliest in history?

a. The United Nations appointed its first Special Rapporteur on Adequate Housing.
b. The United Nations held its first Conference on Human Settlements, or Habitat I.
c. The United Nations declared the International Year of Shelter for the Homeless.
d. The United Nations' Universal Declaration of Human Rights, including to housing.

86. Some home construction companies design houses based on certain principles. Which of the following is a general rule reflecting good design principles?

a. There should be only one way to get to the kitchen.
b. It is better to have several ways to get to any room.
c. Traffic patterns going through rooms disrupt activity.
d. Separate rooms look bigger than in open floor plans.

87. In the interior design of a family home, what is true about the placement of windows?

a. Windows can give good views but no practical benefits.
b. Windows have a tendency to make homes look smaller.
c. Windows are good regardless of number and positions.
d. Windows can create relationships with nature outdoors.

88. When a home construction company advertises new homes as "energy-efficient" or "energy-saving," which of these are the houses most likely to be?

a. Houses built using building principles and techniques that are more energy-efficient
b. Houses built in the traditional/standard way but fitted with energy-saving appliances
c. Houses built to minimize impacts on the environment, regardless of costs or comfort
d. Houses built to reduce energy used by electronics, which consume the most energy

89. What is the Betty Lamp?

a. A modern lighting innovation
b. A colonial lighting appliance
c. It was (B) and is also now (D)
d. The symbol of the AAFCS

90. The AAFCS supports the FCS profession. What is true about its leadership?

a. It works to enhance the well-being of individuals, families, and communities.
b. It influences consumer use of goods and services but not their development.
c. It has a vision and mission to shape social change but not specific public policy.
d. It works to supply leadership to consumers and professionals in all these areas.

91. Which of the following is a division of the AAFCS?

a. The National Association of Teachers of Family and Consumer Sciences (NATFACS)
b. None of these is a division of the American Association of Family and Consumer Sciences.
c. The National Association of Teacher Educators of Family and Consumer Sciences (NATEFACS)
d. The National Association of State Administrators of Family and Consumer Sciences (NASAFACS)

92. As a historical basis relative to gender stereotypes, which of these have been most instrumental in getting women the rights to vote, run for office, inherit and own property, obtain citizenship for their children, and other equal human rights?

a. State institutions
b. Individual women
c. Women's movements
d. (B) and (C) more than (A)

93. How did the Morrill Act (1862) further the domestic sciences in America?

a. By funding industrial colleges with a land grant to teach household management to farm wives
b. By funding industrial colleges with a land grant to teach farm husbands agricultural techniques
c. By funding states with equal land grants for founding agricultural colleges, like with the Turner Plan
d. By funding enforcement of a law banning bigamy and limiting church/nonprofit land ownership

94. How has the United Nations been involved in studying and dispelling worldwide gender stereotypes?

a. The United Nations has not been directly involved with addressing gender stereotypes.
b. Through such groups and actions as an entity for gender equality and panel discussions
c. Only through advisory and technical services that further role models and best practices
d. It has undertaken to examine the impacts of gender stereotypes but not address them.

95. A high school family and consumer sciences class is learning skills to use in job interviews. The teacher asks the students what questions they might ask the interviewer. What student's question would be appropriate?

a. "Will I be able to change my schedule if I'm hired?"
b. "What kind of work is it that your company does?"
c. "Now that we have had an interview, am I hired?"
d. "When would you want me to start if I am hired?"

96. In household management, which of the following would be the first step to take in the process of solving a problem?

a. To identify alternatives among actions
b. To predict outcomes of various actions
c. To collect data concerning the problem
d. To identify what the problem actually is

97. The competency, "Apply a variety of assessment methods to observe and interpret children's growth and development" is found under which of the National Standards for Family and Consumer Sciences?

a. Family
b. Human Development
c. Education and Early Childhood
d. Family and Community Services

98. In the National Standards for Family and Consumer Sciences, under Area of study 8.0, Food Production and Services, which of the following is a competency under Content Standard 8.2, "Demonstrate food safety and sanitation procedures"?

a. "Demonstrate safe and environmentally responsible waste disposal and recycling methods."
b. "Demonstrate professional skills in safe handling of knives, tools, and equipment."
c. "Demonstrate procedures for safe and secure storage of equipment and foods."
d. "Use computer based menu systems to develop and modify menus."

99. Area of Study 10.0, Hospitality, Tourism, and Recreation of the Family and Consumer Sciences National Standards includes Content Standard 10.2: "Demonstrate procedures applied to safety, security, and environmental issues." Which of the following is a competency under this Content Standard?

a. "Apply industry standards for service methods that meet expectations of guests or customers."
b. "Examine lodging, tourism, and recreation customs of various regions and countries."
c. "Apply facility management, maintenance, and service skills to lodging operations."
d. "Demonstrate procedures for assuring guest or customer safety."

100. Area of Study 12.01 of the Family and Consumer Sciences National Standards is Human Development. In this area, Content Standard 12.1 is: "Analyze principles of human growth and development across the life span." Which of the following Human Development Competencies falls under this Content Standard?

a. "Analyze the effect of heredity and environment on human growth and development."
b. "Analyze the effects of gender, ethnicity, and culture on individual development."
c. "Analyze physical, emotional, social, spiritual, and intellectual development."
d. "Analyze the role of communication on human growth and development."

101. Nutrition and Wellness, which is Area of Study 14.0 of the National Standards for Family and Consumer Sciences Education, includes this competency: "Explain physical, emotional, social, psychological, and spiritual components of individual and family wellness." Under which of the following Content Standards does this competency belong?

a. 14.2: "Evaluate the nutritional needs of individuals and families in relation to health and wellness across the life span."
b. 14.5: "Evaluate the influence of science and technology on food composition, safety, and other issues."
c. 14.1: "Analyze factors that influence nutrition and wellness practices across the life span."
d. 14.4: "Evaluate factors that affect food safety from production through consumption."

102. The National Standards for Family and Consumer Sciences Education includes Textiles, Fashion, and Apparel as Area of Study 16.0. In this area, one competency is: "Explain the ways in which fabric, texture, pattern, and finish can affect visual appearance." This competency is found under which of these Content Standards?

a. 16.2: "Evaluate fiber and textile products and materials."
b. 16.3: "Demonstrate fashion, apparel, and textile design skills."
c. 16.4: "Demonstrate skills needed to produce, alter, or repair fashion, apparel, and textile products."
d. 16.7: "Demonstrate general operational procedures required for business profitability and career success."

103. Which of the following is a disadvantage of the laboratory method of learning?

a. The laboratory method uses experience so students learn by doing.
b. The laboratory method enhances learning with multisensory modes.
c. The laboratory method involves more time and expense in learning.
d. The laboratory method gives students preparation directly for living.

104. Of the following, which is an advantage of the demonstration method of teaching?

a. Students can become more passive and dependent.
b. Students can learn best when the classes are smaller.
c. Students can develop observation skills and curiosity.
d. Students can learn but the method takes much time.

105. Business experts find the most important element of total quality management to be effective communication. Which of the following is true about business communication?

a. A company can maintain high quality without good communication.
b. Poor communication leads to interpersonal mistrust in a company.
c. Communication quality has no effect on productivity in a company.
d. Poor communication causes misunderstandings rather than anger.

106. According to some business experts, five kinds of thinking processes are needed for strategic leadership. A leader discerns patterns or connections among abstract ideas and assembles these to create a full picture. This description defines which type of thinking?

a. Intuitive thinking
b. Innovative thinking
c. Conceptual thinking
d. Implementation thinking

107. The FCCLA (Family, Career and Community Leaders of America) student organization helps its members to develop personally through Family and Consumer Sciences education and several areas, e.g., character development and creativity. Among four other areas, which is reflected in a student's evaluating several different insurance policies on multiple features and selecting the most suitable one?

a. Career preparation
b. Critical thinking skill
c. Practical knowledge
d. Interpersonal communication

108. Of the following career information that young people need, which is most likely to help them identify their career interests and preferences?

a. Exposure to higher education and other lifelong learning opportunities
b. Exposure to information on job opportunities that lead to living wages
c. Training in job-seeking skills and in basic workplace skills ("soft skills")
d. Participating in career assessments and job-based exploration activity

109. Which of the following most accurately represents the relationship between FCS educators and Special Education for students with special needs?

a. FCS educators can offer Special Education teachers strategies for teaching life skills.
b. FCS educators' educational preparation typically excludes alternative assessments.
c. FCS educators always need Special Ed. teacher advice on differentiated instruction.
d. FCS educators need Special Ed. teachers for team-teaching special-needs students.

110. Of the following AAFCS resolutions related to public legislation, which is the most recent?

a. Life & Career Choices Class Requirement
b. The resolution about Basic Health Literacy
c. The resolution regarding Healthy Weight
d. 10th anniversary of UN Year of the Family

111. The National Association of Teacher Educators for Family and Consumer Sciences assigned work groups to examine requirements of National Standard 9, Student and Program Assessment, of the National Standards for Teachers of Family and Consumer Sciences. In 2005 these work groups reported four expectations for beginning or pre-service FCS teachers. Which choice accurately reflects one of these expectations?

a. They should know, but not interpret, standards and criteria for FCS programs and student learning.
b. They should collect data about programs and learning using only normed, standardized assessment.
c. They should both reflect and refer to external evidence, but not thereby change teaching practices.
d. They should justify decisions for program design and teaching practices using data-based evidence.

112. For students preparing for careers in FCS, where do food manufacturers have jobs open?

a. Only in product development and marketing
b. Consumer affairs, public policy, and research
c. They need FCS graduates in all of these areas.
d. They have no jobs open in strategic planning.

113. What are some important skills that FCS graduates specializing in fashion design and interior design need to have for working on design teams or operating, managing, and/or owning private design businesses?

a. Their technical knowledge is more important than their creative abilities.
b. They need business expertise, as well as all skills named in these choices.
c. Having global awareness is more important than expertise with business.
d. Creative abilities are imperative whereas other skills are not as important.

114. Which of these is correct regarding what students must do to qualify for a career in FCS?

a. The minimum degree required for employment in the field of FCS is the master's degree.
b. Students must participate in internship programs during 4-year, but not 2-year programs.
c. Additional education courses and practice teaching are required for teaching certification.
d. Graduate work is needed to teach college, do research, or supervise, but not other jobs.

115. What is most accurate about what students should learn about completing job applications?

a. If information is already on résumés they prepared, they need not write it on application forms.
b. They should include all education and experience rather than tailor applications for certain jobs.
c. Details like handwriting, spelling, and following directions matter less than making an impression.
d. They should never lie on job applications, but keeping unfavorable information brief is advised.

116. Which of the following best represents good advice to job applicants for successful interviews?

a. It is good to back up statements about oneself with specific examples.
b. Direct eye contact with interviewers is intimidating and to be avoided.
c. Be prepared to answer interviewer questions but not to ask questions.
d. If one does not understand a question, do not let on and seem foolish.

117. Of the following, which is generally a good practice for writing a résumé?

a. Students with no work history should place education first on a résumé.
b. Education or work history should start with the earliest and go forward.
c. As employers may request personal references, put them in a résumé.
d. In work histories, it is best to include reasons for leaving previous jobs.

118. The AAFCS Code of Ethics holds members responsible for actively avoiding exploiting people with whom they work or interact professionally. In which category of professional practice does the AAFCS place this principle?

a. Professional Competence
b. Respect for Diversity
c. Conflict of Interest
d. Confidentiality

119. The AAFCS expects its members to adhere to its professional conduct principle of Integrity. Which of the following reflects this principle?

a. Protecting private information
b. Making ethically sound decisions
c. Practicing within expertise limits
d. Treating consumers with fairness

120. According to the AAFCS Code of Ethics Statement of Principles of Professional Practice, AAFCS members do not claim to have expertise in areas wherein they are not educated, trained, and experienced. To which of the following principle categories does this relate?

a. Integrity and Confidentiality
b. Professional Competence
c. Respect for Diversity
d. Conflict of Interest

Answer Key and Explanations for Test #2

1. D: Research studies have consistently found that parents are more likely to expect more from their firstborn children. New parents with no previous experience of having their own children are likely to place higher expectations on their first child. By the time they have had more children and experience, they are likely to lower their expectations of their middle (B) and youngest (A) children to be more realistic. Hence most parents are not likely to have the same expectations of all their children (C).

2. C: Researchers have observed that a family's second-born child may take on one of the roles named. A second child often feels s/he gets less attention than the first child and resents being compared to the older sibling. Some rebel against feeling bossed around by the older sibling as well as the parents. Firstborn children (A) are more likely to take on roles of "little parents" by being responsible, conservative, and high-achieving. Middle children (B) tend to play very independent roles and feel relief at less pressure from parents; but also experience less attention, appreciation, and family involvement. Only children (D) may interact better with adults than other children, but are not known to assume the roles named as often as second children are.

3. D: The Family and Medical Leave Act of 1993 requires employers to give qualified employees up to 12 weeks of unpaid leave with their jobs, salaries, and benefits protected for certain medical and family reasons. The law does not specify that this is for maternity leave only (A); or for a choice of either maternity or paternity leave but not both (B); or for both maternity and paternity leave but not for other reasons (C). An employee might take long-term disability leave under this law for an extended illness, and many companies also apply the available duration of long-term disability for maternity and/or paternity leave. Historically, employers gave this leave to new mothers since the law was enacted; and in recent years, companies have increasingly been offering paternity leave to new fathers as well.

4. C: When adults remarry and their respective children are blended into one family, a child's family rank often changes (A); e.g., a child who was formerly the eldest may now be the second or third oldest child, and is treated as such by the rest of family. The roles played by each child also often become less clear (B) than they were in their previous family's dynamics. Additionally, because stepsiblings have no blood relation, incest taboos among them are also less clear-cut (D) than among biological siblings.

5. C: Duvall's Stages of the Family Life Cycle are: (1) childless married couples; (2) families with children 0–30 months; (3) families with children 24 months to 6 years; (4) families with children 6–13 years; (5) families with children 13–20 years; (6) families launching children, from the first child gone to the last child leaving home; (7) middle-age parents, from "empty nest" to retirement; and (8) aging family members, from retirement to both spouses' deaths. The second stage in (A) incorrectly ends with 6 years instead of 30 months. The first stage in (B) incorrectly represents Stage 2 as ending at 6 years instead of 30 months, and the second stage named in (B) represents Stage 4, skipping Stage 3; thus these two are not consecutive. The two stages in (D) are also not consecutive: they name Stages 5, families with teenagers; and Stage 7, middle-age couples from "empty nest" to retirement, skipping Stage 6, families launching children.

6. C: The "later family life" stage is the last stage of some models (cf. Carter & McGoldrick, 1999; Carr, 2006), when family tasks include coping with physical deterioration in oneself and others and with losing spouses and peers; parents' relinquishing, and adult children's assuming, more responsibility to maintain families; and elder members' reminiscing, reviewing their lives, integrating their life experiences, and preparing for death. Helping children develop relationships with their peers (A) is a typical task of the "family with young children" stage. Assuming care for one's family of origin (B) is typically a task during the "family with adolescents" stage. Coping with deaths in one's family of origin (D) is typically a task involved in the stage of "launching children."

7. D: Freud's Oral stage corresponds to infancy, as does Erikson's stage of Basic Trust vs. Mistrust, Piaget's Sensorimotor stage, and Duvall's Families with Infants stage. Freud's Oedipal stage (A) corresponds to preschool; Erikson's corresponding stage is Initiative vs. Guilt, rather than toddlerhood's Autonomy vs. Shame and Doubt; Piaget's Preoperational stage corresponds to preschool, but Duvall's corresponding stage is Families with Preschoolers, not School Age. Freud's Anal (B) stage corresponds to toddlerhood; Erikson's corresponding stage is Autonomy vs. Shame and Doubt, not Industry vs. Inferiority, which occurs during elementary/middle school ages. Piaget's stages corresponding to toddlerhood are the end of the sensorimotor and beginning of the preoperational, not formal operations, which develops around adolescence. Toddlerhood falls between Duvall's Families with Infants and Families with Preschoolers stages. Freud's Genital (C) stage is in adolescence, as is Duvall's Families with Teenagers, but Erikson's corresponding stage is Identity vs. Role Confusion, not infancy's Basic Trust vs. Mistrust; Piaget's is Formal Operations, not the elementary/middle school years' Concrete Operations.

8. D: Freud's Latency stage of psychosexual development corresponds with the elementary and middle school years; therefore, Duvall's family development stage of Families with School-Age Children corresponds most closely to it. Kohlberg's Pre-Conventional stage of moral development (A) corresponds to the preschool years; Freud's corresponding stage is the Oedipal. Erikson's psychosocial stage of Identify vs. Role Confusion (B) and Piaget's Formal Operations stage of cognitive development (C) both correspond to adolescence; Freud's corresponding stage is the Genital.

9. A: Erikson described people undergoing his stage of Ego Integrity vs. Despair in their old age, which corresponds to Duvall's eighth and last stage of Aging Families. Both feature adapting to the process of aging, conducting a life review, and preparing for death as tasks in common for adults. Duvall's Stages VII, Middle-Aged Families (B) and VI, Families as Launching Centers (C), correspond to Erikson's stage of Generativity vs. Stagnation. These share common tasks for adults of leaving legacies to children and grandchildren. Duvall's stage IV, Families with School-Age Children (D), corresponds most to Erikson's stage of Industry vs. Inferiority; both share common tasks for children of meeting new social and academic demands.

10. A: Ainsworth found in her experiments that children with secure attachments to their mothers showed distress when their mothers left the room. She expanded the work of John Bowlby, who defined separation anxiety as a characteristic of normal attachment. Ainsworth found that children she identified as having insecure-ambivalent attachment showed more extreme distress at their mothers leaving than securely attached children, rather than showing no distress (B). However, she found that children she defined with insecure-avoidant attachment showed no distress upon their mothers' leaving the room, rather than showing extreme distress (C). Therefore, children with secure attachment show normal separation anxiety, but this is a lower level of separation anxiety than the level displayed by children with insecure-ambivalent attachment, not higher (D).

11. C: According to Baumrind, the authoritative parenting style is ideal in its combination of high standards, clear expectations, reasoned discipline, and warmth and nurturance. Authoritative parents give children balanced amounts of independence and guidance, respect and love, and firmness and kindness. The permissive (A) parenting style is very loving and warm, but also overly indulgent and lacking in limits, consequences, and control. The authoritarian (B) parenting style is overly controlling and rigid while lacking in warmth. The uninvolved (D) parenting style lacks both warmth and control.

12. C: Baumrind and others after her who have applied her theory in research have found that children who function at low levels in multiple life areas are likely to have had parents with the uninvolved parenting style. This style makes few demands of children, but also demonstrates little warmth toward them. The children thus lack both parental discipline and parental nurturing. Extremes of the uninvolved parenting style include rejecting and/or neglecting children. As a result, children perform poorly and are likely to be depressed and engage in delinquent behaviors. Children with permissive (A) parents are likely to be impulsive, seem immature, lack self-control, and avoid responsibility. Children with authoritarian (B) parents are likely to behave well, but also to lack initiative, avoid leadership roles, and are moody. Children with authoritative (D) parents are likely to be well-behaved but also independent; self-reliant, socially responsible, achievement-oriented, and to have high self-esteem.

13. C: Schaefer's dimensions are (1) along a continuum from warmth to hostility, and concurrently (2) along a continuum from autonomy to control. Comparing these to Baumrind's parenting styles, low control and low warmth equates to her Uninvolved style. Parents with Baumrind's Permissive style (A) have Schaefer's high warmth, but also high autonomy, not low. Parents with Baumrind's Authoritarian style (B) have Schaefer's high hostility, but also high control, not low. Parents with Baumrind's Authoritative style (D) have a balance of Schaefer's dimensions: enough but not excessive (i.e., intrusive, codependent) warmth; sufficient control to set reasonable limits and enforce rules consistently, but not so much to be rigid or overly punitive; enough autonomy to let children make their own decisions and learn from their mistakes, but not so much to leave children without the structure and guidance they need. While high warmth with high control (A) in Schaefer's model does not correlate with a Baumrind parenting style, this combination is often characterized as "smother love."

14. B: Bandura said that in order for modeling of behaviors to be effective, the four conditions of attention, retention, reproduction, and motivation were necessary. Attention (A) requires the observational learner to attend to the behavior modeled. Degrees of attention are affected by multiple variables like the functional value of the behavior, its complexity, distinctiveness, prevalence, and affective valence (how emotionally attractive the observer finds it), and the observer's level of arousal, sensory capacities, perceptual set, and having received past reinforcement for similar behaviors and/or for observing others' behaviors. Motivation (B) is most related to the observers' having good reason(s) for observing and imitating others' behaviors, e.g., previous rewards, imagined or promised rewards, and vicarious; i.e., observing others being rewarded for behaviors. Retention (C) involves being able to remember the behaviors one observed. Reproduction (D) involves imitating or replicating the observed behavior.

15. B: Traditional behaviorists believed that an individual's environment caused the individual's behaviors (A). Bandura proposed that not only do the individual's behaviors also cause the environment (C), which he *reciprocal determinism;* i.e., the environment and the behaviors mutually determine one another, but moreover that the individual's psychological processes (D) also interact with environment and behavior to produce learning and shape the personality. Thus he did not believe that any one of these factors caused any other(s), but that all three reciprocally interact and influence each other.

16. C: In his theory, Maslow proposed a progressive hierarchy of needs, often illustrated in a pyramid: He proposed each level of needs must be met before any higher level(s). The most basic needs essential to survival, which must be met first, are at the pyramid's base/bottom. Maslow termed these physiological needs, e.g., food, water, and sleep. As these come before all others, (A) is incorrect. At the pyramid's point/tip/top, Maslow placed "self-actualizing needs," i.e., to fulfill one's highest potentials. These can only be realized after all other needs lower on the pyramid are met; hence (B) is incorrect. Maslow placed "security needs," i.e., for shelter and safety, second after physiological needs (C). Needing to feel love, affection, and belonging, i.e., what Maslow called "social needs" are third in his hierarchy; what he termed "esteem needs," i.e., to have self-esteem and feel personal worth, social recognition, and accomplishment are fourth. Hence (D) is incorrect.

17. D: When parents divorce, the family structure is necessarily changed; this is the most direct and obvious effect. However, it is very common for divorce also to change the family's income (B): One parent may have custody of all children but half the income of the couple or less; when couples split custody among several children, the parents' two households may have unequal incomes; divorce court-ordered child support and alimony may be less or more than the previous income of the couple; some parents fail to pay the ordered child support, etc. Community expectations (C) are also often affected: divorce can change where family members live, their types of homes, and where the children attend school; this in turn can cause neighborhood pressures on a family. All of these factors can change the family dynamics.

18. B: One of many benefits of family recreation researchers have found is that it improves communication within the family. Teaching moral values and healthy lifestyles (A) is a benefit researchers have found family recreation provides children as individual members of the family; providing children with educational experiences (C) is another. Fulfilling the diverse needs (D) of different family members is more of a challenge to planning and engaging in family recreation that researchers have found, rather than a benefit of family recreation to either the family group or individual family members. (Of course meeting the needs of all family members would be a benefit of family recreation when this is actually accomplished; however, researchers have not identified it as a benefit but a challenge, because it is so difficult to achieve with no existing universal structure for programming family recreation.)

19. D: Erikson's stage of Generativity vs. Stagnation occurs in middle adulthood, when people focus on creating legacies to leave for future generations, such as children, businesses, homes, inventions, and other contributions to family and society. Those who stagnate rather than generate become self-absorbed. Intimacy vs. Isolation (A) occurs in young adulthood, when people either succeed at forming intimate relationships with others or become isolated from them. Ego Integrity vs. Despair (B) occurs during old age, when people review their lives and feel either satisfaction or regret. Identity vs. Role Confusion (C) occurs during adolescence, when teens either succeed at establishing a personal identity or become confused about what their role is.

20. B: Gesell characterized the ages of 2 years, 5 years, 10 years, and 16 years as times when children's development is marked by balance (equilibrium), consolidation of abilities, and emotional smoothness or stability. He described the ages of 2½, 5½ to 6, and 11 years (A) as times when children's previous patterns are breaking up, resulting in disequilibrium and more difficult behaviors. Gesell characterized the ages of 3½, 7, and 13 years (C) as times when children are internalizing and integrating things: 3½-year-olds show unbalanced physical coordination and emotional insecurity, while 7-year-olds and 13-year-olds tend to rebel and/or withdraw. He described the ages of 4, 8, and 14 years (D) as periods when children's development is marked by "vigorous, expansive" movement toward the outside world.

21. B: Havighurst included in developmental tasks he defined of middle age (35 to 60 years) the need to adjust to the physiological changes that occur with aging. He included adopting civic responsibilities (A) as a developmental task of early adulthood (18 to 35 years). He included meeting social and civic obligations (C) as a developmental task of later life (60 years and older). He included developing socially responsible behaviors (D) as a developmental task of pre-adolescence and adolescence (12 to 18 years).

22. D: Piaget named a unilateral (B) or one-sided morality and adult-child relationship, based on obedience to authority, heteronomous or controlled by others. He named an independently constructed morality, and an adult-child relationship of reciprocal respect, as autonomous. The adult coerces the child in the heteronomous relation and "co-operates" (i.e., collaborates in performing operations) with the child in the autonomous one, rather than vice versa (A). The autonomous relation involves interaction and cooperation whereas the heteronomous involves adult constraint of the child rather than the opposite (C).

23. D: In infancy (A), Maslow's first level of Physiological needs takes priority. In adulthood (B), people may give priority to any or several of his needs levels depending on their circumstances. However, assuming they have met all the other levels, adults are most likely to be concerned with the highest level of self-actualization needs. In adolescence (C), the third and fourth levels of need, for love and belonging and for esteem, are likely to have priority. Whereas infants are most concerned with meeting their needs to sleep, be fed, changed, etc., in toddlerhood the emphasis typically progresses to meeting their needs for safety and security.

24. B: Children in the early school years, e.g., from four to six years old, have developmental tasks including learning to play in groups, identifying with a gender role, and early moral development. Toddlers (A), e.g., from two to four years old, have developmental tasks including locomotion beyond toddling; symbolic representation and pretend play; developing language; and learning self-control. Children in middle school (C), e.g., from six to twelve years old, have developmental tasks including making friends; performing concrete mental operations; learning academic and social skills; participating as a team member in playing games; and evaluating themselves. Infants (A), e.g., from birth to two years old, have developmental tasks including motor, perceptual, and sensory maturation; basic emotional development; social attachment; sensorimotor cognition; understanding basic causation, objects, and categorizing.

25. A: The developmental tasks named are characteristic of early adolescence, around the ages of 12 to 18 years old. Typical developmental tasks in later adolescence (B) include establishing one's sex role identity, becoming independent of one's parents, developing an internalized moral sense, and making career choices. Typical developmental tasks at middle school age (C), around six to 12 years old, include forming and maintaining friendships; performing concrete mental operations; learning academic and social skills; self-evaluation; and engaging in team play. Typical developmental tasks in early adulthood (D) include starting to work at a job, getting married, and having children.

26. C: It is more typical for adults to develop a perspective regarding death in later adulthood than in old age when closer to death (D). By old age they usually have already established a point of view about death and are occupied with reviewing their lives, adjusting to the deaths of spouses, etc. Young adults (A) are typically engaged in other developmental tasks like marrying, starting families, and working. Middle-aged adults (B) are typically involved in tasks like developing their marriages, households, and careers and parenting their children.

27. B: A common characteristic in autism spectrum disorders is not understanding others' social cues, and hence also not using those cues to communicate socially. For example, an autistic individual might not understand that another person's smiling indicates happiness and/or friendliness, and may feel these emotions but not realize that smiling communicates them to others. Attentional deficits (A) are special needs more commonly associated with ADHD. Autistic people are more likely to focus intensely on one activity or subject for prolonged times. Motor control and coordination difficulties (C) are more common in developmental disabilities like cerebral palsy. (Autistic people may engage in odd-looking and/or repetitive movements, but this is not a motor difficulty.) Many autistic individuals adhere very rigidly to consistent routines rather than having difficulty with doing so (D); with autism, it is commonly a bigger problem if that routine is disrupted, which can cause "meltdowns"; or if someone wants to convince the autistic person to change a routine.

28. C: Certain types of spina bifida cause paralysis. The vertical location of the defect in spinal column closure dictates how high the paralysis occurs: in some patients the bladder and bowels are affected, while in others it may be limited to the feet and lower legs. A common symptom is inability or difficulty in walking. Communication boards (A) are for people who cannot speak for cognitive (e.g., intellectual disability) or neuromuscular (e.g., cerebral palsy) reasons or vocal system disorders. Text-to-speech software (B) is also for people who cannot speak normally, including those with autistic disorders, deafness, ALS, etc. Cochlear implantations (D) are to restore hearing for those with sensorineural hearing loss.

29. D: What Bronfenbrenner named the exosystem represents the wider social system, including such factors as local and global communities, community resources available to the child's family, the work schedules of the child's parents, etc., that affect the child's development. The chronosystem (A) is what Bronfenbrenner called the temporal system that affects the child's environment, including processes and events like the child's physiological maturation, cognitive development, or parental deaths, divorces, and other experiences that alter development and life. The microsystem (B) is Bronfenbrenner's term for the interactions and relationships a child has with people in the family, neighborhood, school, and other environments. The mesosystem (C) is what Bronfenbrenner called the connection between parts of the microsystem, such as between parents and teachers, etc. (Bronfenbrenner also identified the macrosystem, meaning the system of beliefs, values, laws, customs, and other cultural influences on the child.)

30. D: Freud theorized that young boys unconsciously desired their mothers and wanted to get rid of their fathers as competition for the mother's attentions. He called this the Oedipal conflict after the Greek character who unknowingly killed his father and married his mother. While Freud omitted girls from this concept, neo-Freudians following him expanded it to include the Elektra conflict. Just as Freud said boys resolved the Oedipal conflict by wanting to be just like and emulating their fathers (C), neo-Freudians said girls resolved the Elektra conflict by wanting to be just like their mothers and imitating them. This is called "identification with the aggressor" because the child unconsciously fears retaliation by the same-sex parent for his or her aggressive impulses. Neither Freud nor the neo-Freudian psychologists believed girls just grow out of (A) the conflict. Symbolically "killing" the mother (B) is not how girls resolve the conflict; it is rather the impulse to do so that they resolve by identifying with the mother.

31. C: Toman found in his research that an oldest child, who grew up being comfortable with a leadership role, will have a complementary relationship in the workplace with an assistant who grew up as a youngest child and is more comfortable with following the leader. (Youngest children may also like being in charge, but usually have different leadership styles than oldest children.) A boss and assistant who both grew up with the same sibling positions {(A), (B)} are more likely to clash by being too similar in motivations and styles. A boss who was a youngest child and an assistant who was an oldest child (D) are less likely to have as effective a relationship, as their respective roles are more likely mismatched to their interactional personality characteristics.

(Murray Bowen also incorporated Toman's findings into his Family Systems Theory, making it better known.)

32. C: Distractors are described by Satir as those members who divert the others' attention from problematic issues and the attendant emotions by engaging in various attention-getting behaviors. Distractors may be the "babies" of their families, and feel the others will only love them if perceiving them as harmless and cute. Blamers (A) hide their insecurities by attacking the others. Placators (B) try to appease the others to avoid the rejection or disapproval they fear. Computers (D) avoid confronting or expressing feelings by denying all emotion and limiting their communication to only intellectual, objective, or factual topics.

33. B: Sender-oriented values are characteristic of low-context communication, wherein the speaker is responsible for the clarity of his or her communication, rather than the listeners having responsibility for understanding it (C). This does not mean the speaker ignores the values of the listeners (A). In low-context communication, which has sender-oriented values rather than interpreter-sensitive values (where the listener is responsible to understand), the speaker uses direct patterns of verbal orientation rather than indirect patterns (D), which are used in high-context communication.

34. A: Like gestures and other nonverbal channels of communication, eye contact is a culturally dependent orientation. It is not viewed the same universally across all cultures (B). For example, in Japan, listeners prefer indirect eye contact with speakers and avoid prolonged or direct eye contact (C). Even in the USA, where direct eye contact is considered more important while speaking, public speakers are still advised to make direct eye contact with only some audience members but use indirect eye contact with others (D) according to their individual preferences. In America, knowing which audience members prefer direct or indirect eye contact is a skill required for public speaking.

35. D: While increasing globalization means that cultures are mixing and communicating more, this does not mean that nonverbal forms of communication have become more universally similar (C). It means rather that people are exposed to more culturally dissimilar forms of nonverbal communication, requiring speakers to become more aware, observant, and sensitive to these cultural differences. People generally assume nonverbal communication to be more truthful than verbal communication, not vice versa (A). Humor *is* classified among the major areas of nonverbal communication (B), as are areas like paralinguistics, proxemics, gestures, posture, body language, facial expressions, eye contact, etc.

36. A: This example suggests ("may," "if," "try") rather than insisting, as with "must" (B), "only one way to do that right" (C), or negating as in "doing it wrong" (D). Example (A) not only offers a mild suggestion, which the recipient is more likely to accept; it also frames the advice as being in the recipient's best interest. The other examples do not; instead, they give commands, implying that the speaker assumes power over the recipient. The recipient is more likely to reject or resist these as attempts at coercion. The form of communication in (A) is more likely to promote cooperation and prevent conflict; those in the other choices are more likely to promote defensiveness and/or conflict.

37. D: Erikson's theory of psychosocial development is the only one of the three named whose stages include young adulthood, middle adulthood, and old age until death. Freud's and Piaget's theories both have stages that end with adolescence. Freud's theory of psychosexual development ended with adolescence because he believed the personality was essentially formed by then. Piaget's theory of cognitive development ended at adolescence because he believed his highest stage of Formal Operations was attained by then. (Later researchers have found some adults never attain it.) Of the three, only Erikson included adult developmental stages in his theory.

38. D: Having access to information that supports better purchasing decisions is an example of the consumer's right to education. Minimizing environmental impacts through purchasing choices (A) is an example of a consumer's *responsibility* to promote a healthy environment. An example of the consumer's *right* to a healthy environment is to reside and work in environments that are not detrimental to the consumer's health. Following safety instruction to ensure the safe use of products (B) is an example of a consumer's *responsibility* for safety. An example of a consumer's *right* to safety is to be protected against health hazards in products and services. Sustainable consumption that will not impinge on others' needs (C) is an example of a consumer's *responsibility* to meet basic needs. An example of a consumer's *right* to have basic needs met is to have access to shelter, water, and food.

39. D: The provision of the Wall Street Reform and Consumer Protection Act of 2009 that consumers can sue credit rating agencies for negligence fulfills the consumer's right and responsibility concerning redress, i.e., to request compensation for an agency's wrongdoing. This law's provision that brokers have the same fiduciary duties as advisors if they give investment advice to consumers (A) fulfills the consumer's right to be given accurate product information, and the responsibility to analyze and apply that information judiciously; and the consumer's right to have access to education to inform purchasing decisions, and the responsibility to pursue consumer education about products as they change. The law's provision that advisors disclose information to the SEC on request (B) also fulfills the consumer's right and responsibility to information [see (A) above]. The law's provision of protection to whistleblowers (C) fulfills the consumer right and responsibility to be heard.

40. A: The FTC was established by the administration of President Woodrow Wilson in 1914 through the FTC Act and the Clayton Act as the anti-trust legislation of the New Freedom. 1934 (B) was when the Securities and Exchange Commission (SEC) was established under the administration of President Franklin D. Roosevelt to regulate the stock market and securities industry; the SEC took over enforcement of the Securities Act from the FTC, which originally enforced it before SEC formation. Three of five initial SEC commissioners came from the FTC, one of whom later became SEC Chairman. 1979 (C) was when the FTC charged the American Medical Association (AMA) with anti-competitive practices by unlawfully limiting consumer information access on medical service availability and prices, restricting employment on the salary of doctors by hospitals and other facilities, and banning advertising. (The FTC's orders that the AMA revoke these restrictions were then upheld by court ruling.) 1995 (D) was when the FTC established its website, www.FTC.gov.

41. A: According to research, consumers who have not formed any preconceived notions about the quality of various providers through what they have heard from others, through advertising they have seen/heard, or through their own prior experiences are more interested in price as a factor in their health care decisions. However, when consumers have traditional health insurance plans, like PPOs or HMOs (B), they are less interested in price because these plans control price. When consumers have severe or urgent medical conditions (C), they are less interested in price because obtaining immediate care takes priority. And when they like their current health care practitioners (D), they are less interested in price because they want to see the same provider(s) regardless.

42. C: The quality of a product or service—or how useful it is, how durable, etc.—is classified as soft information, which individual consumers vary in judging. In other words, soft information is subjective. Hard information is objective because it is made up of facts. For example, the weight (A) of a product; the price (B) of a product or service; or the contents (D) of a product (e.g., the ingredients in food, cosmetic, or cleaning products) are all facts and hence are examples of hard information.

43. A: Since income tax must be paid, for financial planning purposes one should use after-tax income to determine how much is available to pay living expenses and debts. Using gross income before taxes (D) is unrealistic for paying bills as part of that money goes to paying taxes. Taxpayers either have taxes withheld from their paychecks by their employers, or pay estimated taxes in advance quarterly if self-employed, or pay their total tax for past year when filing their tax returns, etc. Living expenses and debts are NOT the same thing (B): they are two separate categories. Living expenses include mortgage or rent, utilities, food, health care, etc. Debts are accumulated amounts already owed rather than new monthly bills, like credit card debt, outstanding medical bills, loan repayment, etc. Assets listed *should* include savings (C) as these fit the definition of an asset, whether one plans to spend them or not.

44. C: It can help for other people to recommend financial goals (A), especially for young people about to be graduated from high school or college and/or starting jobs. However, though others can give advice about goals, they should not tell the individual which ones to pursue (B); this is something the individuals must decide for themselves. Financial goals can include savings, investments, and spending as well (D). If someone has a goal to buy a house, car, business, etc., these are included as financial goals, so spending can be as much a part of a person's financial goals as saving and/or investing to provide for financial security and/or freedom in the future.

45. B: By law, clothing manufacturers are required to include all of this information on the labels, tags, packaging, or printed on the inside of the fabric: a registered ID number identifying the manufacturer (A); the country where the clothing was made (C); the fiber content of the garment; and the care instructions, which are also required and not optional (D).

46. D: Nutrition Facts panels on food packaging are required by law to include the serving size, number of servings per container, calories per serving; grams of protein, carbohydrates, fats, and fiber per serving; milligrams of sodium per serving; and the percentage per serving of the Daily Value for protein, carbohydrates, fats, cholesterol, and also certain vitamins and minerals.

47. D: Calcium is among several minerals and vitamins whose amounts are represented in Nutrition Facts as a percentage of the Daily Value (based on a 2,000-calorie per day diet according to the FDA, and on a 2,500-calorie a day diet according to the USDA). Unlike vitamin and mineral supplement packages, food packages do not show calcium in number of milligrams (A). Calcium in supplements is commonly measured in milligrams, not in micrograms (B) as Vitamin D is measured, but this measurement is not shown on food labels. The amount is not shown as a percentage of a serving size (C) of the food, but as a percentage of the Daily Value (DV), i.e., the percentage of how much calcium is recommended in the daily diet. For example, given a DV of 1,000 mg of calcium, the label of an 8-ounce milk container will show its calcium content as 30% rather than as 300 mg.

48. C: The cognitive bias based on representativeness occurs when a manager makes a decision based on wrongly generalizing about something that only happened once, or about a sample that is too small to be representative of an entire group. The prior hypothesis bias (A) occurs when a manager makes decisions based on beliefs s/he has previously formed about a relationship among factors, even though these beliefs are proven wrong by the evidence. The illusion of control bias (B) occurs when a manager overestimates how much s/he is able to control what will happen. The escalating commitment bias (D) occurs when a manager has already committed significant resources to a project, and then after problems with it are revealed through feedback, commits even more resources to it in an attempt to resolve the problems.

49. B: In the devil's advocacy method, one alternative at a time is presented by the group, and one group member then critiques the alternative and/or the group's process for identifying alternatives by pointing out the drawbacks. In the dialectic inquiry method, two groups each select alternatives and each group then critiques the other group's choices. Managers listen to each group's presentation and critique of alternatives. Thus the number of alternatives presented at a time is one with devil's advocacy and two with dialectic inquiry. With both methods, alternatives are reassessed (A) after being critiqued and/or debated. With both methods, an alternative may be accepted (C). With devil's advocacy, if not accepted the alternative will be rejected or modified; with dialectic inquiry, if both alternatives are not accepted, only one may be accepted; or the two may be combined. With both methods, increasing group diversity has the same effect (D): a broader range of alternatives becomes available with more diverse members contributing.

50. B: The 80/20 Rule means that 80% of our typical work activities contribute less than 20% to the value of the work we do. Therefore, if we only complete the 20% of our tasks that are most important, we still realize the majority of the value from our work. This rule is one of the primary reasons why prioritizing is an effective tool for time management. Choices (A), (C), and (D) are NOT correct definitions of the 80/20 Rule.

51. C: The eldercare.gov site helps consumers find elder-care facilities in their local communities. Typing one's ZIP code or city and state into the designated box yields a list of local facilities or one may search by topic (e.g., Alzheimer's Disease, Caregivers, Elder Abuse Prevention, Financial Assistance, Food & Nutrition, Health Insurance, Home Repair and Modification, Transportation, Volunteerism, and others). Medicare's website (A) offers an overview of options for long-term care, a tool for comparing Medicare- and Medicaid-certified nursing homes, and more. The LeadingAge website (B) gives consumers information on what to look for when taking tours of prospective nursing homes. LeadingAge is part of the International Association of Homes and Services for the Aging (IAHSA). The website of the Assisted Living Federation of America or ALFA (D) also provides consumers with a checklist to use when visiting prospective nursing homes.

52. C: Due to the recent economic recession (c. 2007–2009), many child caregivers are now offering multiple services, like housekeeping, tutoring, etc. Parents can thus get help in more areas for their money. Also because of the recession, many caregivers are charging *lower* rates, not higher (A). Another recent trend owing to economic factors is *more* parents getting help with child care from their own parents (B). (Fewer extended families lived together in the recent past than historically, but this is changing.) Some families relocate to live with/nearer to their parents, or invite their parents to live with/closer to them. This offers dual advantages of saving money on child care, and helping grandchildren and grandparents get better acquainted. Au pairs, i.e., foreign nationals, typically cost *less* in wages because parents provide their room and board as well, but State Department regulations limit their service to one-year periods, preventing longer-term provider continuity for young children. Hence regulations are a bigger challenge than wages with au pairs, not vice versa (D).

53. D: The government's Energy Star website is best because it lists all home appliances and equipment with Energy Star labels for meeting EPA-set energy-efficiency specifications, and includes annual electricity and water use, free of charge. The Sears website (A) is good for consumers who want to buy specifically from Sears, because they can type "Energy Star appliances" into the site's search bar and it will display all Energy Star products sold by Sears. The Energy Star.gov site is better by not restricting customers to one store for buying energy-efficient home equipment and appliances. McGraw-Hill's Sweets Network site at http://products.construction.com/ (B) is an excellent site, but only for locating construction materials and building products and equipment; it does not sell appliances. The Consumer Reports website (C) rates and recommends appliances among many other products, including whether they meet Energy Star requirements; however, while consumers can read its buying guides online, they must pay for a subscription to view the actual ratings, including Energy Star information.

54. B: Experts recommend that parents choose toys that stimulate both creativity and social interaction. They advise toys that both boys and girls can play with are better (A)—which also saves money for parents with both. Experts recommend toys that stimulate several senses rather than just one at a time (C). And they find that eye-hand coordination and problem-solving skills are equally important for toys to develop, rather than one over the other (D).

55. B: All of these accurately describe women's nutritional requirements. Women differ from men not only in numbers of calories, but also in the amounts they need of various nutrients. And even among women alone, their nutritional needs will not be the same at different times during their menstrual cycles (C), or when they are pregnant, or when they are breastfeeding (nursing) infants (D).

56. D: A significant portion of American adults consume more sodium (A) than is recommended. This has been associated with an increase in the number of adults who develop hypertension, or high blood pressure, which can threaten an individual's cardiovascular health. Many American adults consume less than the recommended amount of calcium (A), fiber (B), and vitamin D (C). Deficiencies in these nutrients can lead to health complications, but overconsumption of sodium is most closely associated with hypertension.

57. B: Vitamin C increases the body's absorption of non-heme iron, i.e., iron from plant sources such as beans, tomatoes, prunes, spinach, pumpkins, etc. Calcium (A), vitamin D (C), and vitamin E (D) are not known to increase the absorption of iron from vegetables, fruits, and legumes.

58. C: A 1.4-oz. (40-gram) chunk of cheddar cheese has 296 mg of calcium. A 4.2-oz. (120-gram) slice of fruit cheesecake has 94 mg of calcium. A 5.3-oz. (150-gram) serving of plain low-fat yogurt has 243 mg of calcium. A 2.6-oz. (75-gram) serving of plain vanilla ice cream has 75 mg of calcium. So the yogurt is second to the cheddar cheese, the cheesecake is third, and the ice cream is fourth.

59. B: Vitamins A, D, E, and K are fat-soluble vitamins, meaning they dissolve in lipids, i.e., fats. The body absorbs these vitamins in fat globules and stores them in the tissues. Therefore, if someone ingests excessive amounts of any of these vitamins, they can build up to harmful levels. Vitamin C (A) and the complex of B vitamins (C) are water-soluble vitamins, meaning they dissolve in water and are not stored in the tissues. Any excess amounts are excreted in urine and sweat. Water-soluble vitamins do not build up in the body, but fat-soluble vitamins do. Therefore (D) is incorrect.

60. D: The USDA recommends that in a healthy meal, at least half of the plate should be made up of fruits and vegetables. Its recommendations for proteins (A) vary by age, sex, and activity level from 2 ounces to 6 ounces daily. Most Americans eat enough protein; but the USDA advises eating a greater variety of proteins, and leaner ones. Recommendations for grains {(A), (C)} also vary with age, sex, and activity from 3 to 8 ounces daily, but the USDA advises at least half of all grains we eat should be whole grains rather than refined grains. USDA recommendations for dairy foods {(B), (C)} depend on age: 2 cups daily for ages 2–3 years, 2½ cups daily for ages 4–8 years, and 3 cups daily for ages 9 years and older.

61. B: %Daily Values (DVs) make it easier for consumers to know how much of what they need daily of certain nutrients a food supplies. For example, if a food contains 33%DV of sodium, the consumer knows that food supplies 1/3 of the sodium s/he should consume in a day. This means consumers need *not* know the actual numerical amounts of nutrients they need daily, or how much of that number a food has (A); e.g., they need not know that 2400 mg of sodium is how much to consume daily, or that a food with 800 mg of sodium has 1/3 the DV. %DVs also make it *easier* for consumers to comparison shop, not harder (C); e.g., they can pick a food lower in sodium instead of one with too much. The FDA developed DVs *not* because the RDAs were inaccurate (D), but because certain nutrients the FDA wanted to require on labels did not have RDAs established for them.

62. C: By definition, bulimia is a disorder wherein the patient binge-eats excessive amounts of food and then purges it by inducing vomiting, abusing laxatives, or both. Anorexia (B), a disorder wherein the patient starves, eating almost no food, and often also exercises excessively, *sometimes* but *not always* also includes binge-eating and purging, or just purging. Therefore, (A) and (D) are incorrect.

63. B: In type 1 diabetes, the pancreas does not produce insulin, the hormone necessary for converting sugars, starches, and other foods to energy. In type 2 diabetes, the pancreas does produce insulin, but the body does not respond properly to the hormone; this is called insulin insensitivity. Both type 1 and type 2 diabetes have both genetic and environmental factors, so (A) is incorrect. While type 1 diabetes was previously called "juvenile diabetes," it can develop in childhood or young adulthood; and though most cases of type 2 diabetes used to develop during adulthood, in recent years many children and adolescents have been diagnosed with type 2 diabetes, so (C) is incorrect. Type 1 accounts for only 5% of diabetes cases while the rest are type 2, so (D) is incorrect.

64. B: One tip from nutrition experts for healthy eating is to exercise instead of eat to relieve boredom. While eating should be interesting and enjoyable, it should be done out of hunger, not boredom. Experts do advise keeping a log or diary of what foods we eat, when we eat them, why, etc. Keeping records does *not* cause obsession or compulsion (A), it is the other way around: people with obsessive-compulsive disorder or prone to obsessive-compulsive tendencies may think obsessively and behave compulsively about anything, including keeping eating records. Keeping track of eating helps most people understand their eating habits and change them if needed. Experts advise *not* skipping meals (C), which can cause unstable blood sugar levels, fatigue, and subsequent overeating. Experts also advise people *not* to prohibit themselves from ever eating certain foods, even those considered unhealthy (D). This encourages abnormal attitudes toward food and bingeing on either the forbidden foods or allowed ones.

65. C: One component of CBT is breaking linkages or associations between eating/food and other things when those connections contribute to overeating, emotional eating, poor food choices, etc. Some techniques for breaking linkages include not eating in certain environments; not keeping poor food choices at home; finding alternatives to eating as coping mechanisms; obtaining social support; changing eating habits; using positive reinforcement, problem-solving strategies, rehearsal, etc. Another component of CBT involves positive self-statements (A), used to replace self-defeating thoughts (e.g., "I'll never change," "This is too difficult," etc.). Evaluating readiness for change (B) is a component of CBT wherein the individual becomes aware of what s/he needs to do to attain his/her weight management goals, and then commits to doing those things. Self-monitoring (D) is a component of CBT wherein one keeps track of things like food choices, portion sizes, and factors other than hunger that trigger eating. This increases eating self-awareness and supports focusing on long-term success.

66. A: When planning the menu for a meal, one should first decide what the entrée should be, as it is the "centerpiece" of the meal. The planner should then decide upon what side dishes (B) will go well with the entrée. The décor (C) should also be chosen to complement the entrée rather than vice versa. The menu should be planned first, and then the foods needed should be bought rather than buying foods first and then designing a menu to include those foods (D).

67. B: Dining etiquette dictates that hosts and guests should pass dishes to the right, not clockwise (A) with the exception of bread, which should be passed clockwise; hence (C) is incorrect. The rule for cutting up one's food is to cut up anything larger than one's thumb at the second joint rather than being up to the individual guest (D).

68. A: Food poisoning can be caused by all of these preparation factors with certain foods. For example, cooking for the wrong lengths of time (B) and/or at the wrong temperatures (C) can cause perfringens food poisoning due to the microorganism *clostridium perfringens*. Unpasteurized milk can cause illness from the bacteria *campylobacter jejuni; salmonella; E. coli* O157:H7 infection; and/or *listeria monocytogenes;* and unrefrigerated (or improperly refrigerated) meats, cream pastries, and egg or potato salads with mayonnaise can cause food poisoning from the bacterium *Staphylococcus aureus.*

69. A: Microwave ovens are by far more energy-efficient than the others named, in both cooking efficiency and energy factor. (Cooking efficiency equals the fraction of the total energy the oven consumes that is used to cook food. Energy factor equals the ratio of energy used for cooking food to the total energy consumed.) Convection ovens (B) powered by electricity are more energy-efficient than convection ovens powered by gas; and both kinds of convection ovens are more energy-efficient than traditional electric or gas ovens; but a microwave oven is about 7–8 times more energy-efficient than electric or gas convection ovens, about 5 times more efficient than standard electric ovens, and about 9–10 times more efficient than regular gas ovens. (Note that efficiency refers to energy used, not cost in money, which depends on local rates charged for electricity and gas.)

70. A: Partially hydrogenated vegetable oil is produced through a chemical reaction of liquid vegetable oil with hydrogen to make it semi-solid, as in shortening. This process creates trans fats, which contribute to heart disease. The US FDA has found trans fats even more dangerous than saturated fats. These fats raise LDL (low-density lipoproteins) or "bad" cholesterol, which clogs arteries, and lower HDL (high-density lipoproteins) or "good" cholesterol, which helps remove "bad" cholesterol from the arteries. They also promote inflammation. Fully hydrogenated vegetable oil (B) does not contain trans fat and seems harmless, as its saturated fat is converted to monounsaturated fat by the body. Monounsaturated fats (C), like olive oil, canola oil, peanut oil and peanut butter, sunflower oil, sesame oil, avocados, and many other seeds and nuts, lower LDL, can raise HDL when replacing saturated fats, decrease inflammation, and supply antioxidants that combat diseases. Polyunsaturated fats (D) like regular, nonhydrogenated vegetable oils, lower total cholesterol and LDL, and can raise HDL when replacing saturated fats.

71. A: Freeze-dried cheese is a good way to have cheese in long-term storage for emergencies, etc. However, it does cost more than fresh cheese does. Hence (B) is incorrect. Food storage experts do not recommend using freeze-dried cheese regularly to replace fresh cheeses (C). Rather, to ensure one's comfort with using it, they recommend trying it in a few of one's favorite recipes. There are two ways to reconstitute freeze-dried cheese. The quicker method—placing it on paper towels, spraying with water, stirring, and waiting—is fine for melting the cheese and using it in recipes. The method that takes longer—drizzling cold water over it in a bowl while stirring continuously, and then refrigerating in a zip-lock bag for several hours to overnight before use—rehydrates the cheese to be just like fresh cheese; hence (D) is incorrect.

72. C: Wardrobe experts advise individuals to use "tough love" on their closets and get rid of anything they have not worn for more than a year (A), anything that does not fit them (B), and anything that is not consistent with their personal styles (D) rather than only one of these. For those who can afford it, experts recommend that if they cannot bear to part with many such items and/or have trouble deciding which things to get rid of, to employ a personal stylist for help.

73. D: Everybody has a certain group or family of colors that are most flattering to them based on their skin tones. Experts advise getting rid of clothes with colors outside of this group as we do not look as well in them (A). They also advise keeping and buying clothes whose colors all coordinate, which makes it easiest to mix and match items into different outfits and gives the largest potential numbers of outfits we can create (C). Keeping items in less flattering colors just to provide more variety or a change of pace (C) is not the best advice, because we do not look as well wearing colors we may like to see but which don't flatter us. Others respond less favorably to us when we wear unflattering colors, and we are likely not to feel as good about how we look when we wear them.

74. A: Many color analysts use the four seasons to identify the main categories of color palettes. In this system, "Autumn" represents warm, yellow-based earth tones; "Winter" represents cool, blue-based colors and black and white; "Spring" represents bright, vibrant, clear colors; and "Summer" represents soft, light pastel tints of colors. Some color analysts use adjectives descriptive of temperaments for the same groups. In this system, "Passionate" equals "Autumn"; "Dramatic" equals "Winter"; "Vibrant" equals "Spring"; and "Romantic" equals "Summer."

75. D: An A-line skirt is widest at the hem, balancing out full hips without excess fabric to make the figure look bigger. The full profile of a circle skirt (A) can make the hips look even fuller and accentuate the thinness of thin legs below the hem. A pencil skirt (B) has a narrower hem and fits closely overall; this would exaggerate the contrast between full hips and thin legs. A fishtail skirt (C) is very narrow around the knees and then flares out below the knees. While this would disguise skinny legs, it would also magnify full hips.

76. C: Woven fabrics can be made using a plain weave, a twill weave, a satin weave, or a triaxial weave. In the plain weave, one yarn alternates going over and under the other. The two yarns at right angles are called the warp (A) and the weft (B). In the twill weave, the weft goes under and over two or more warp yarns at regular intervals. In the satin weave, each yarn goes over four or more others before crossing under another one. The low twist and long "float," or distance yarn goes between crossings, make satin smooth and shiny. In the triaxial weave, yarns go in three directions instead of only two. In addition to a warp and weft, the third yarn direction is called the whug (C). Woof (D) is not a weaving term. (In audio electronics, e.g., speakers and amplifiers, tweeters transmit high sound frequencies and woofers transmit low frequencies.)

77. B: Unfinished knitted or woven fabrics are first cleaned to remove dirt and oils from the manufacturing process. Then many fabrics are singed with heat to eliminate protruding ends of fibers, which prevents fabric pilling and promotes even color when dyeing. After singeing, cotton and other natural fibers are bleached to get rid of impurities in their natural color and appearance. Fabrics that do not respond well to bleach are treated with optical brighteners instead. Manufacturers may then Mercerize certain linens, cottons, and rayons using alkali to make them stronger, softer, more lustrous, and more readily accepting of dyes. Fabrics are then dyed to add colors.

78. D: The fabric care symbol of a square with an arc resembling a slightly slack clothesline hanging from between the top corners indicates the garment should be line-dried or hang-dried. The symbol of a square with diagonal lines in the upper left corner (A) indicates the garment should be dried in the shade (i.e., not in direct sunlight if this would fade the dye). A square with one horizontal line inside (B) indicates the garment should be dried flat. A square with three vertical lines inside (C) indicates the garment should be drip-dried.

79. C: When people buy houses with mortgages, they usually make a down payment in some amount; however, this is not always required (A). Buyers usually pay closing costs as well, but also not always (B). There are some loan programs that allow the borrower to purchase a house with no money down; and in buyers' markets (i.e., when the housing market affords the buyer more leverage), realtors can help buyers negotiate deals wherein the owner or seller pays some or all of the closing costs. While some buyers want to eliminate a down payment, many others prefer to pay something down to lower their subsequent monthly mortgage payment: paying nothing down results in higher monthly payments (D).

80. A: In the real estate business, it is most common for some realtors to represent buyers and others to represent sellers. Realtors typically do not represent both {(B), (C)}. This does not typically vary by the individual realtor (D), as realtors usually represent either home buyers or home sellers.

81. B: Realtors usually advise consumers to obtain pre-approval before they decide to bid on a particular house for several reasons. For example, through the pre-approval process, consumers can meet in person or online with different lenders and learn about various loan options; this helps them discover how much money they can afford to spend (A) and which loan programs will meet their needs best (C). Another reason that realtors suggest obtaining pre-approval is because purchase forms for real estate commonly stipulate that the buyer applies for financing within 7 to 10 days or some other limited period of time. It can be difficult to locate a lender and undergo a credit check that quickly, and the time pressure can cause consumers to make poor financing decisions. However, if they have found loan officers and loan programs ahead of time, it is much easier to make a well-informed decision and complete a financing application within the time limit.

82. C: One might assume that the term "first-time buyer" refers to anybody who has never owned any real property before (A), but this is not true in the realty market. In most US states, this term actually refers to anyone who has not owned property within the past three years. It does not refer to anyone who has owned real estate property for less than six months (B), or to anyone who once owned but does not currently own any real estate property (D).

83. A: Today, consumers can apply for mortgage loans from diverse sources including mortgage bankers and mortgage brokers, but these are not the only sources (B); they can also apply at savings and loan associations, credit unions, commercial banks, mutual savings banks, and insurance companies (C); and today, more and more realtors are also able to arrange mortgage financing for home buyers (D).

84. C: Home buyers need to get home warranty and insurance coverage at the closing of the sale. Thus they should consult an insurance broker or a realtor before the closing to get information and make choices. It is too late to obtain insurance after the closing (A), but too early when making a bid on a house (B) since the home buyer does not know yet if s/he will end up buying the house when bidding. It would also be premature to obtain insurance when applying for a mortgage (D), which the buyer should do before making an offer for a specific house to the seller.

85. D: The UN issued its Universal Declaration of Human Rights, which includes the right to adequate housing, in 1948. The UN appointed its first Special Rapporteur on Adequate Housing (A) in 2000. The UN held its first Conference on Human Settlements, which it called Habitat I (B), in 1976. (Its second Conference on Human Settlements, called Habitat II, was held in 1996.) The UN declared the International Year of Shelter for the Homeless (C) in 1987.

86. B: One design principle embraced by some home design companies is that there should be at least three ways to get to a room in the house. They find this especially important for getting to the kitchen, which is the center of many family homes; therefore (A) is incorrect. Floor plans can be designed wherein people get to different rooms by passing through other rooms in an open floor plan, yet without disrupting how the rooms are used (C). These open floor plans make the rooms look bigger than if they were separated by halls (D) used as passageways. They also make it easier to see farther through the house.

87. D: Windows in a home can form connections to the natural environment outdoors, which also improve home experiences indoors. In addition to beautiful views when they are in the right places, windows also yield practical benefits (A) by letting in natural sunlight and fresh air. By letting in light and allowing people to see out, windows create the perception that rooms and houses look bigger, not smaller (B). However, architectural designers also need to consider factors like whether a window opens on an unattractive view, interferes with homeowners' privacy, faces in a direction that does/does not let in light at the wrong time(s) of day, etc. Therefore they must know how many windows to include and where to place them most appropriately (C) to achieve the best effects.

88. A: Concerns over climate change and protecting our environment has prompted many construction companies to research building science principles to make new houses more energy-efficient. These houses are not built in traditional ways but simply containing energy-saving appliances (B); rather, they reduce the use of energy in the house greatly from the use in a house built, for example, seven years ago. These new houses are built not only to minimize the carbon footprint, i.e., the environmental impact, of those living in them; they are also built to cost homeowners less in energy expenses and to make living there more comfortable for them (C). Building scientists find that heating and cooling are what consume the most energy in houses, not electronics (D).

89. C: The Betty Lamp is not a modern lighting innovation (A). Rather, it was a lamp widely used during colonial times in early America, which gave a relatively good quality of light for the time. Because this lamp was historically used to light not only family life, but also all household industries, and because it could represent the enlightenment that the American Association of Family and Consumer Sciences (AAFCS) is dedicated to providing, the AAFCS adopted it as its official symbol (D) in 1926.

90. D: The AAFCS states that its leadership works not only to enhance the well-being of individuals, families, and communities (A), but also to influence how consumer goods and services are developed, delivered, and evaluated (B), and to influence both general social change and specific public policymaking (C).

91. B: None of these organizations is a part of the AAFCS. All three of them are parts of the Association for Career and Technical Education (ACTE), the biggest national education association in America dedicated to preparing young and adult people for career success through advancing education. However, the AAFCS and ACTE are related in that the ACTE has a division devoted to family and consumer sciences, of which (A), (C), and (D) are all sections.

92. D: As researchers point out and history confirms, individual women (B) such as Susan B. Anthony, Elizabeth Cady Stanton, and others, and the women's movements (C) they started have been more instrumental in fighting for and winning women's rights than state institutions (A) have been. In a similar vein, some researchers propose that national policy and law must be more proactive to undo gender stereotypes.

93. A: The Morrill Act funded land grants to US states to create agricultural colleges. This law did enable these colleges to educate farmers in agricultural techniques (B); however, the way it furthered domestic sciences in America specifically was by enabling these same colleges to educate the farmers' wives in household management (A). The Turner Plan, written by Illinois College's Professor Jonathan Baldwin Turner, gave states equal land grants for agricultural colleges. However, the Morrill Act, also written by Turner and introduced by Vermont congressman Justin Smith Morrill, did *not* allocate *equal* land grants to all states (C), but grants of variable sizes according to how many congressional representatives and senators each state had. This favored the eastern states, which had larger populations. The Morrill *Anti-Bigamy* Act, also passed in 1862 by President Abraham Lincoln, banned bigamy and limited church/nonprofit land ownership (D), targeting the Utah Territory's Mormons; however, its enforcement was *not* funded; Lincoln never enforced it; and it did not further domestic sciences.

94. B: The United Nations has UN Women, the UN Entity for Gender Equality and the Empowerment of Women. UN Women has held panel discussions, such as in Geneva (2011) on countering negative gender stereotypes and discrimination as part of its Economic and Social Council (ECOSOC)'s session. The UN also includes the Commission on the Status of Women (CSW). It states the UN General Assembly (UNGA), CSW, and ECOSOC "have been addressing this issue over time and need to continue to keep a vigil, and strengthen norms to change the cosmography of gender stereotyping." The UN's 2011n panel aimed not only to examine gender stereotyping's impact, but also to combat it and to identify "effective policies and norms." Therefore (D) is incorrect. The UN's advisory and technical services not only further role models and best practices, but also "implement, monitor and evaluate programmes," and these services are in addition to "advocacy, knowledge brokering, strategic partnerships including with CSOs, media and private sector." Thus (C) is incorrect.

95. D: Of the choices given, the most appropriate question to ask in a job interview would be when the employer would want the applicant to begin work if hired because it relates directly to the job and reflects a realistic consideration. Asking about changing his or her schedule if hired (A) could reflect a less than responsible attitude, which could negatively influence the interviewer. Asking what kind of work the employer does (B) would betray the applicant's lack of preparation and information about the company, which s/he should have researched before the interview. Asking whether s/he is hired (C) during the interview, even at its end, would be premature because hiring decisions are often made only after all applicants have been interviewed, or at the least after that applicant's interview rather than during it, and would moreover place the interviewer in an awkward position.

96. D: Problem-solving skills are among the critical thinking skills needed not only for academic activities, but also in real life including household management. Consumer and family sciences teach these. The first thing necessary to solve a problem is to identify what the problem is. Identifying different actions that could be taken (A); predicting what the results of those actions might be (B); and collecting information related to the problem (C) depend on, and cannot be done without, first defining the specific problem to be solved.

97. C: The competency quoted is Competency 4.2.2 under Content Standard 4.2, "Analyze developmentally appropriate practices to plan for early childhood, education, and services" under National Standard 4.0, Education and Early Childhood, whose comprehensive standard is, "Integrate knowledge, skills, and practices required for careers in early childhood, education, and services." The standard for Family (A) is National Standard 6.0, whose comprehensive standard is, "Evaluate the significance of family and its effects on the well-being of individuals and society." Human Development (B) is National Standard 12.0, whose comprehensive standard is "Analyze factors that influence human growth & development." Family and Community Services (D) is National Standard 7.0, whose comprehensive standard is "Synthesize knowledge, skills, and practices required for careers in family & community services."

98. A: "Demonstrate safe and environmentally responsible waste disposal and recycling methods" is Competency 8.2.10 under Content Standard 8.2, "Demonstrate food safety and sanitation procedures". "Demonstrate professional skills in safe handling of knives, tools, and equipment" (B) is Competency 8.5.1 of Content Standard 8.5, "Demonstrate professional food preparation methods and techniques for all menu categories to produce a variety of food products that meet customer needs." "Demonstrate procedures for safe and secure storage of equipment and foods" (C) is Competency 8.3.5 of Content Standard 8.3, "Demonstrate industry standards in selecting, using, and maintaining food production and food service equipment." "Use computer based menu systems to develop and modify menus" (D) is Competency 8.4.1 of Content Standard 8.4, "Demonstrate menu planning principles and techniques based on standardized recipes to meet customer needs."

99. D: "Demonstrate procedures for assuring guest or customer safety" is Competency 10.4.6 of Content Standard 10.4, "Demonstrate practices and skills involved in lodging operations." "Apply industry standards for service methods that meet expectations of guests or customers" (A) is Competency 10.3.1 of Content Standard 10.3, "Apply concepts of quality service to assure customer satisfaction." "Examine lodging, tourism, and recreation customs of various regions and countries" (B) is Competency 10.5.1 of Content Standard 10.5, "Demonstrate practices and skills for travel related services." "Apply facility management, maintenance, and service skills to lodging operations" (C) is Competency 10.4.6 of Content Standard 10.4, "Demonstrate practices and skills involved in lodging occupations."

100. C: "Analyze physical, emotional, social, spiritual, and intellectual development" is Competency 12.1.1 of Content Standard 12.1. "Analyze the effect of heredity and environment on human growth and development" (A) is Competency 12.2.1 under Content Standard 12.2: "Analyze conditions that influence human growth and development." "Analyze the effects of gender, ethnicity, and culture on individual development" (B) is Competency 12.2.3, also under Content Standard 12.2 (above). D. "Analyze the role of communication on human growth and development" (D) is Competency 12.3.2 under Content Standard 12.3: "Analyze strategies that promote growth and development across the life span."

101. C: This competency is Competency 14.1.1 of Content Standard 14.1, "Analyze factors that influence nutrition and wellness practices across the life span." An example of one competency under Content Standard 14.2, "Evaluate the nutritional needs of individuals and families in relation to health and wellness across the life span" (A) is Competency 14.2.1: "Analyze the effect of nutrients on health, appearance, and peak performance." Under Content Standard 14.5, "Evaluate the influence of science and technology on food composition, safety, and other issues" (B), an example of one competency is Competency 14.5.1: "Analyze how scientific and technical advances influence the nutrient content, availability, and safety of foods." Under Content Standard 14.4, "Evaluate factors that affect food safety from production through consumption" (D), an example of one competency is Competency 14.4.1: "Analyze conditions and practices that promote safe food handling."

102. B: The competency quoted is Competency 16.3.1 under Content Standard 16.3, "Demonstrate fashion, apparel, and textile design skills." Under Content Standard 16.2, "Evaluate fiber and textile products and materials" (A), an example of one competency is Competency 16.2.2: "Evaluate performance characteristics of textile fiber and fabrics." Under Content Standard 16.4, "Demonstrate skills needed to produce, alter, or repair fashion, apparel, and textile products" (C), an example of one competency is Competency 16.4.5: "Demonstrate basic skills for producing and altering textile products and apparel." Under Content Standard 16.7, "Demonstrate general operational procedures required for business profitability and career success" (D), an example of one competency is Competency 16.7.1: "Analyze legislation, regulations, and public policy affecting the textiles, apparel, and fashion industries."

103. C: One disadvantage of instruction using the laboratory method is that lab experiments and other procedures consume more time than other learning methods, and the apparatus used in labs can be very expensive. The experiential nature of the lab method means that students learn by actually doing things instead of by reading about or being told about them, which is an advantage (A). Students generally learn better when they receive material through multiple sensory modalities; this is another advantage of the lab method (B). An additional advantage of the lab method is that through hands-on experience and discovery, it prepares students directly for many processes they will encounter in real life (D).

104. C: One advantage of the demonstration method of instruction is that watching the instructor actually perform a process, conduct an experiment, etc., both stimulates their curiosity to learn how things are done and also sharpens their skills of observation. Other advantages include that it is systematic; it wastes less in resources, effort, and time than when students experiment themselves; and it avoids the trial and error process students often undergo when doing it themselves. Disadvantages of this method include that students can become more passive by being observers than when they actively engage in hands-on learning, and can become more dependent on the teacher to show them things (A); demonstrations work best with small classes (B), but many classes are so large they make demonstrations ineffective; though students learn from demonstrations, the teacher's instructions and actual demonstration are very time-consuming (D); and the teacher must have sufficient expertise for an effective demonstration.

105. B: Research into business communication has demonstrated that poor communication in an organization eventually causes individual employees to mistrust each other. This research also shows that poor communication undermines quality (A); compromises productivity (C); and causes not only lack of understanding among members, but also development of anger (D) among individuals in an organization. Researchers conclude that the difference between profit and loss, or between success and failure, in a business is most often attributable to whether communication in the business is effective or not. These findings are the reasons that experts identify effective communication as the most important element of total quality management in business.

106. C: Some business experts say that five types of thinking processes are needed for strategic leadership: Critical thinking, implementation thinking, conceptual thinking, innovative thinking, and intuitive thinking. The description given defines conceptual thinking. Intuitive thinking (A) involves being able to perceive or sense some truth without any external supporting evidence or information, and to apply this perception appropriately as a factor in making the ultimate decision. Innovative thinking (B) involves being able to generate new approaches and/or ideas that produce useful opportunities and possibilities. Implementation thinking (D) involves being able to structure plans and ideas such that they can and will be carried out effectively.

107. B: Being able to analyze multiple features objectively, evaluate several different plans based on that analysis, and make a decision informed by the evaluation is an example of critical thinking, which is one of the areas whereby the FCCLA helps its members develop life skills. This example does not reflect the area of career preparation (A) because it does not involve learning job skills, identifying career interests, or making career choices. It does not reflect practical knowledge (C) as much as such examples as knowing how to stay within a budget, drive a car, do laundry, cook a meal, etc. It does not reflect interpersonal communication (D) as the student's process of analysis, evaluation, and decision-making did not necessarily involve communicating with other persons.

108. D: All of these choices reflect ways that young people can gain information on the career options available to them. Among them, the choice most likely to help them specifically identify their career interests, preferences, and goals is to participate in career assessments and in job-based exploration activities like visiting actual job sites and job shadowing (following specific employees and/or positions to learn what they do in their jobs). Career assessments help reveal the areas where students have the most aptitude and interest; and work-based exploration activities help students gain firsthand experience to identify which kinds of work they find most appealing.

109. A: FCS educators can be valuable resources for Special Education teachers by offering them consultation, team-teaching with them, and offering them strategies for teaching life skills to students with special needs. FCS educators typically are aware of alternative assessments (B) and differentiated instruction (C). Rather than their requiring Special Education teachers for team-teaching special-needs students (D), FSC educators can more often meet the needs of Special Education teachers for instructing special-needs students in Family and Consumer Sciences education by team-teaching with them.

110. C: The AAFCS' Healthy Weight Resolution was issued in 2011 to support national nutrition education and obesity prevention. The AAFCS made a resolution that a class in Life and Career Choices should be required in middle schools and junior high schools (A) in 2007. The AAFCS issued a resolution supporting education and policies that promoting health literacy (B) in 2010. The AAFCS resolved in 2003 that the 10th anniversary of the United Nations International Year of the Family should be observed (D) in 2004.

111. D: Four expectations the NATEFCS work groups identified for beginning or pre-service FCS teachers were that they *should* be able to interpret standards, criteria, and processes for evaluating FCS programs and student learning (A); that they should collect data about program effectiveness and student learning outcomes using *varied* assessments, *including* performance assessments and authentic assessments, not only normed, standardized assessments (B); that they should not only engage in personal reflection and refer to evidence from various external sources, but moreover *should* adjust their teaching practices based on this information (C); and that they should use data-based evidence to justify their decisions about program design and teaching practices (D).

112. C: Currently, food manufacturers have positions they need to fill in product development, marketing (A), consumer affairs, public policy, research (B), and strategic planning (D). Graduates of FCS programs will be most qualified to fill these positions, so food manufacturing companies hope these graduates will apply for jobs in their industry.

113. B: Today's FCS graduates who specialize in fashion and interior design must have a combination of technical knowledge, creative abilities {(A), (D)}, global awareness, and business expertise (C) for working on design teams or operating, managing, and/or owning private design businesses. No one of these is more important than the others.

114. C: Students majoring in FCS who want to become teachers will need to take additional courses in education and also do practice teaching in order to obtain a teaching certificate. The minimum degrees required for employment in the FCS field are the associate's degree or the bachelor's degree, not the master's (A). FCS students are expected to participate in internship programs in *both* four-year and two-year curriculum programs (B). FCS students will need to pursue graduate education for careers in not only teaching college, doing research, and supervising, but *also* in food and nutrition, and in teaching at extensions and in other extension jobs (D).

115. D: Students should learn never to lie on job applications; however, experts do advise that regarding experiences or events that could cast applicants in an unfavorable light, they should be as brief as possible. If employers are interested in the candidate, they will schedule an interview, wherein they can ask for more details. Students learning how to fill out job applications should also learn to fill in all requested information on the forms even if it is already on the résumé they will attach, rather than leaving it off the application (A). Students should learn to research the companies where they are applying; and it can help to tailor their application responses to emphasize the education and experience that fit a certain job best (B). Neat handwriting, correct spelling, and following directions on application forms *do* matter, and in themselves make as favorable an impression as sloppy writing, misspelling, and not following directions make an unfavorable one (C).

116. A: One good piece of advice for job applicants preparing for interviews is, when answering questions about themselves, they should support statements they make about their own positive attributes with specific examples to illustrate those qualities whenever they can. However, it is not good advice to avoid eye contact with interviewers (B). This would be good advice in Japan, where direct eye contact is found intimidating and is avoided; but in America, it is a sign that one is paying attention and is interested in the conversation. Avoiding eye contact in job interviews in America can be interpreted as a lack of confidence or as dishonesty. Applicants should be prepared not only to answer questions, but also to ask them (C). Applicants can ask interviewers what the company is looking for in an employee; interviewers' responses can provide applicants with opportunities to explain how they meet those needs. If applicants do not understand an interviewer question, they should not try to hide it (D), but rather should request clarification.

117. A: In résumés, those with work experience should place their job histories first; students with no work history should place their educational histories first. When writing one's educational or work history in a résumé, one should list the most recent item first and work backward, not vice versa (B). One should NOT include personal references in the résumé itself (C). For employers who request personal references, the applicant should submit these separately. Résumés should NOT include reasons for leaving previous jobs (D). If these are relevant, they can be addressed during job interviews.

118. C: The principle of not exploiting people is under the Conflict of Interest category of the AAFCS Principles of Professional Practice in its Code of Ethics. The Professional Competence (A) category includes principles related to credentials; professional development; education, training, experience; claims of competence; and practice within legal limits. The Respect for Diversity (B) category pertains to practices that support diversity and respecting differences in cultural beliefs and backgrounds. The Confidentiality (D) category covers trust, respect, cooperation and confidentiality, and protecting people's confidential information in professional relationships.

119. B: Making ethically sound decisions is a principle under the Integrity heading of the AAFCS Code of Ethics Principles of Conduct. Protecting private information (A) is a principle under the Confidentiality heading of these principles. Practicing within the limits of one's expertise (C) is a principle under the Professional Competence heading. Treating consumers, as well as colleagues, individuals, and families, with fairness (D) and avoiding divided loyalties is a principle under the Conflict of Interest heading.

120. B: In the AAFCS Code of Ethics, in its Statement of Principles of Professional Practice, the category of Professional Competence includes the principle that "AAFCS members claim competence in area(s) for which they have education, training, and experience." The only concept that overlaps across the principles of Integrity and Confidentiality (D) and Conflict of Interest (A) is that of avoiding exploitation. Respect for Diversity (C) does not involve claims of competence, but rather having respect for and supporting differences among people's beliefs, backgrounds, and cultures.